FOUNDATIONS OF ACCOUNTING THEORY

Papers given at the
Accounting Theory Symposium
University of Florida
March 1970

Edited by
WILLIARD E. STONE

University of Florida Press
Gainesville / 1971

University of Florida Accounting Series No. 7

LIBRARY OF CONGRESS
CATALOG CARD NO. 75–137855
ISBN 0–8130–0314–8

PRINTED IN U.S.A.

Bill Paton, Shirt Sleeves Accountant

THE PROCEEDINGS of the accounting theory symposium on "Foundations of Accounting Theory" held on the University of Florida campus in March 1970 are dedicated to Dr. William A. Paton.

His influences on accounting theory beginning in 1922 with *Accounting Theory* have continued undiminished for a generation. It was William A. Paton who first formulated an integrated, viable theory of accounting which dared to depart from the pragmatic, work-a-day approach. So many of his innovations have now been accepted, both in theory and in practice, that it is difficult to remember the storms of controversy raised by his ideas in earlier years. The academic phase of accounting theory, in particular, owes much of its progress of recent years to the firm foundation provided by Dr. Paton's work.

It is a pleasure and an honor to dedicate the proceedings to Dr. Paton as a very small recognition of the enormous debt which the profession of accounting owes to him.

Gainesville
1970

WILLIARD E. STONE

Honored Guest

William A. Paton

Participants

Albers, Wayne J., Ernst & Ernst
Anderson, Carl A., University of Florida
Anderson, Wilton T., Oklahoma State University
Benninger, Larry J., University of Florida
Bhada, Yezdi K., Ohio University
Brown, James E., Stetson University
Caplan, Edwin H., University of New Mexico
Clift, R. C., University of Melbourne
Copeland, Ronald M., Pennsylvania State University
DaVault, James W., University of Florida
Demaris, E. Joseph, University of Illinois
Devine, Carl T., Florida State University
Ellett, John S., II, University of Florida
Fertig, Paul E., Ohio State University
Flowers, William B., University of Alabama
Frank, Werner, University of Wisconsin
Gorton, Donald E., Wayne State University
Green, David, Jr., University of Chicago
Haas, Robert S., Lybrand, Ross Bros. & Montgomery
Hartman, Robert F., Jr., Florida Technological University
Hendricksen, Eldon S., Washington State University
Horwitz, Bertrand, Syracuse University
Jergensen, Louis C., University of South Florida
Keller, Thomas F., Duke University
Langendorfer, Harold Q., University of North Carolina
McCullers, Levis D., University of Kentucky
Miles, Catherine E., Georgia State University
Miller, Herbert E., Michigan State University
Mobley, Sybil C., Florida A & M University
Montgomery, James B., Florida Atlantic University
Mueller, Gerhard G., University of Washington
Patten, Ronald J., Virginia Polytechnic Institute
Pattillo, James W., Louisiana State University
Pointer, Larry G., Texas A & M University
Price, Harry R., University of Miami
Ray, Delmas D., University of Florida
Schattke, Rudy, American Institute of CPAs
Stone, Williard E., University of Florida
Thorne, Jack F., University of Florida
Voss, William M., University of Arkansas
Whitehurst, Frederick D., University of Florida
Williams, Thomas H., University of Texas
Wixon, Rufus, Wharton School, University of Pennsylvania
Wyatt, Arthur R., Arthur Andersen & Company
Yeargen, P. B., University of Georgia
Yu, Shih Cheng, University of Florida

Contributors

NORTON M. BEDFORD, Ph.D., CPA, holds the Weldon Powell Memorial Professorship in accountancy, and is Professor of Accountancy and Business Administration, College of Commerce and Business Administration, University of Illinois (Urbana-Champaign). He was also President of the American Accounting Association at the time of this symposium.

R. J. CHAMBERS is Professor of Accounting, University of Sydney, New South Wales, Australia, and was Visiting Professor of Accounting, University of Florida, in 1970.

C. WEST CHURCHMAN, Ph.D., is Professor of Business Administration, Schools of Business Administration, University of California (Berkeley).

HARVEY T. DEINZER, Ph.D., CPA, is Professor of Accounting, College of Business Administration, University of Florida.

LOUIS GOLDBERG, Litt.D., is Head of the Department of Accounting, University of Melbourne, Melbourne, Australia, and was Visiting Professor of Accounting, University of Florida, in 1970.

ROBERT E. JENSEN, Ph.D., is the Nicolas M. Salgo Professor of Operations Research, College of Business Administration, University of Maine.

Kermit D. Larson, Ph.D., CPA, is Associate Professor of Accounting, College of Business Administration, University of Texas (Austin).

Alfred Rappaport, Ph.D., CPA, is Associate Professor of Accounting and Information Systems, Graduate School of Management, Northwestern University.

Robert T. Sprouse, Ph.D., is Professor of Accounting and Director of the Stanford Executive Program, Graduate School of Business, Stanford University.

Robert R. Sterling, Ph.D., is Professor of Business Administration, School of Business, University of Kansas.

John T. Wheeler, Ph.D., is Professor of Business Administration and Associate Dean for Academic Affairs, Schools of Business Administration, University of California (Berkeley).

Stephen A. Zeff, Ph.D., is Professor of Accounting, Graduate School of Business Administration, Tulane University.

Contents

Introduction

William A. Paton

I'M ESPECIALLY PLEASED to have the opportunity to make these comments, as in my status of "honored guest" at the meetings where these papers were presented there seemed to be no appropriate point at which I could put in my oar.

First, I'd like to remind readers that the rubric for the conference, according to the printed program, was "Foundations of Accounting Theory." And on the outside cover appeared the related caption "Accounting Theory Symposium." With such headings one would expect to hear *something* about accounting, and I am glad to be able to report that several speakers did actually deal with accounting and its basic problems. They were perhaps outnumbered—if commentators are included—by those presenting a somewhat hazy mixture of the "new" approaches and points of view, embroidered with a dab of statistics and mathematical allusions and occasional references to the amazing developments in computers and other devices, but the group addicted to plain accounting saved the day by keeping the conference at least within sight of the course laid out for it. Providing major help in this connection were the outstanding presentations of the professors from "Down Under," Ray Chambers and Lou Goldberg.

Right here I must confess that I get very tired at times of what the current crop of revolutionaries in accounting have to say, especially those who find excuses for abandoning or avoiding the term "accounting" entirely. I don't object particularly to the content of their statements, but I don't like the pretension that they have broadened horizons and made discoveries of great importance. Actually they are ruminating, with little added but some fresh jargon. See, for a major example of earlier explorations, the extensive writing of Dr. Leon Carroll Marshall, and especially his proposals at meetings of the American Association of Collegiate Schools of Business, during his tenure as dean of the College of Commerce and Administration at the University of Chicago (1909–1924). Marshall was all for suppressing accounting altogether through glorification of quantitative measurement, broadly defined, and through statistical approaches and techniques. It should also be noted that the need for servicing management, of which so much is made nowadays, was stressed by Marshall and many of his contemporaries. Indeed, the view that a major objective of accounting is facilitating the administration of business has always accompanied systematic study of the subject, from the earliest days.

Accounting is a broad and pervasive field, as business transactions of every kind that are expressed in monetary terms are our meat and drink. But this doesn't mean that the accountant must be a mathematician, a statistical wizard, a psychology specialist, a rhapsodic social participant, or even a computer operator (although here's an area that he must be keenly aware of). I heartily go along with Ray Chambers when he suggests that we will do well to confine our attention to something less than the whole field.

For a long time I've wished that the Paton and Littleton monograph ("An Introduction to Corporate Accounting Standards") had never been written, or had gone out of print twenty-five years or so ago. Listening to Bob Sprouse take issue with the "matching" gospel, which the P & L monograph helped to foster, confirmed my dissatisfaction with this publication. As I look on this monograph now, I surmise that the authors must have been unduly influenced by one of FDR's famous fireside chats in which he stated: "I am going to put prices back at the 1926–1929 level and then hold them there for a generation" (this is from memory, unverified). The basic difficulty with the idea that cost dollars, as incurred, attach like barnacles to the physical flow of materials and stream of operating activity is that it is at odds with the actual process of valuation in a free competitive market. The customer does not buy a handful of classified and traced cost dollars; he buys a product, at prevailing market price. And the market price may be either above or below any calculated cost figure. Despite any statements in the monograph that seem to hold otherwise, I have never espoused the socialistic, cost-plus interpretation of product pricing, and I apologize, humbly, for any apparent veering in this direction contained in Paton and Littleton. On the other hand, we have to admit that costs must be recognized and dealt with. Probably we can agree that orderly and reasonable procedure in the final absorption of costs incurred is preferable to purely arbitrary, haphazard treatment.

For a long time I've been touting the idea that the central element in business operation is the *resources* (in hand or in prospect) and that the main objective of operation is the efficient utilization of the available assets. I am further firmly convinced that the most significant measure of any resource is what it is currently worth (not always readily determinable, I'll grant). How can we determine where we stand, what earning rate we are achieving, or where we should go from here without knowing the value of employed resources? I object, vigorously, to certified statements showing land and timber at a fraction of their demonstrable current market value, with no mention of the true facts anywhere. Several speakers at the conference, I am happy to report, took note of the importance of current market values.

With respect to the present-day emphasis on prediction, I was greatly impressed with Professor Chambers' position, indicated in the following quotation: "I can readily admit the necessity of future calculations; but I cannot see how these calculations can be made, or if made, can be worthwhile, without the fullest possible knowledge of the present financial state of the firm and the fullest possible account of its past."

In concluding these scattered comments, I can't forego the opportunity to pay tribute to my longstanding and esteemed friend Professor Williard E. Stone. Who but Will Stone would have had the audacity to conceive of this conference, and who but he would have displayed the persistence and ingenuity necessary to bring such a project to an impressive fruition. Hearty congratulations to you, Williard!

Information, Business, and Society

Norton M. Bedford

IF THERE IS ANYTHING to the total systems approach, it would appear that some set of relationships ought to exist among information, business, and society. It would seem that business activities must depend on the information supplied the business entity and that the nature of society must depend significantly upon the actions taken by business. Contrariwise, it would seem that the nature of society will condition significantly that which business does and that the activities business decides to undertake will determine the type of information which needs to be supplied. Thus it appears that there must exist something of a network or a system which flows from information to business to society and back again. Furthermore, it would appear that accountants, representing the main business-information system of American society, ought to be interested in the nature of the set of relationships implied by such a network. The development of such a set of relationships in detail and the construction of a network display of their interconnections are, of course, well beyond the capacity of human accomplishments in the present and foreseeable future. Consequently, one must paint with a broader brush and in subdued, rather than bold, colors. Nevertheless, there is a great need for such a painting if the accounting discipline is to adapt to this changing world.

Without such a picture, no matter how indistinct the pattern outline, there exist no acceptable criteria for expanding the scope of accounting technology and the area to which that technology should be applied.

Let us start the picture of the network with the notion of information. While it has many definitions, the rather crude one that "information is a bit of news that reduces a decision-maker's uncertainty as to the decision he ought to make or the action he ought to take" will suffice for this analysis. Recall that this means that communicating to a decision-maker something already known would not be information, nor would disclosing a bit of news not bearing on the decision under examination qualify. By inference, if information reduces uncertainty, then misinformation would increase a decision-maker's uncertainty as to the decision he ought to make or the action to take. Furthermore, the nature of man's imagination is such that there is ample reason to think that misinformation, as well as information, is a well-established institution in most societies of the world. In fact, there seems to be such a considerable amount of misinformation floating around in society that any analysis of information ought to include an examination of the nature of misinformation and its impact on business and society.

One more notion must be set forth before starting an analysis of the relationships among information, business, and society. It is the concept of "environmental instability," which is essentially a subjective concept because environment is merely that view of the outside world entertained by a decision-maker over which he believes he has no control. It includes the economic conditions of a society, the political philosophy prevailing within and among nations, and every other exogenous constraining factor perceived by the decision-maker. Because these environmental factors seem to an individual decision-maker to fluctuate in a rather random manner, they represent nonconstant factors which the decision-maker views as environmental instability. In addition, if a decision-maker is confronted with an exogenous factor of which he had not previously been aware, he thinks of the environment as unstable, because it does not present itself to him in terms of specific known factors. In view of these two conditions, it appears that the environmental instability faced by a decision-maker may be increased either by making the decision-maker aware of previously unconsidered factors in his environment or by, in fact, increasing the fluctuations of the factors comprising his known environment. To the decision-maker, both of these developments would result in an increase in the complexity of the environment in which he views himself as acting. To the decision-maker, changes in the instability of his environment represent changes in the complexity of the environment in which he is operating. In this sense, the complexity of an environment refers to the difficulty of perceiving and being aware of all elements in the environment and the way these elements interact. Complexity could be increased or decreased by changing the number of significant factors in the decision-maker's environment or by changing the extent of interactions among these factors.

For an individual decision-maker, it is the instability of the environment that makes decision-making difficult. Because he can never be completely informed, to the individual decision-maker the environment is more of an unstable factor than it is a complex factor. But, on the average, for all decision-makers this instability varies directly and is highly correlated with the complexity of the environment. This is significant, for, at the macro level, with which this study is concerned, it is environmental complexity rather than environmental instability with which the accountant needs to be concerned.

The advantage of shifting to the macro level is that the study shifts from the multitude of individual subjective views of environmental instability of each decision-maker to an average condition, which at any point in time is a single, valued condition. There is no way of knowing, of course, what this average condition of environmental instability is; in fact, there is no need to know, for our interest is concerned primarily with changes in the average and only incidentally with what it is at any one point in time.

Changes in environmental instability, you will recall, were due either to the decision-maker becoming more aware of previously unconsidered factors in his environment or to an actual increase in the instability of the perceived environment. The shift to the macro level excludes the first of these from consideration, because, "on the average," man's intelligence will not change so rapidly that there will be a sudden overall increase in man's intuitive perception of the nature of his environment. Rather, without formal information-development processes, it appears that man's ability to comprehend his existing environment occurs slowly. This means that, if a study is seeking to determine the relationships among information, business, and society at only a general level, it is appropriate to ignore the gradual intuitive increase in the intellectual capacity of man to understand his environment. This does not mean that this factor must be ignored. If one is more rigorously inclined, there is certainly no reason not to develop a rate of change in man's ability to understand the environment in which he operates and then add this to the change in the complexity of the previously known environment. For the purpose of starting this analysis, however, it is assumed that at the macro level the bulk of the changes in the instability of the environment are due to changes in the actual complexity of that environment. These changes in the complexity of the environment are technological and social value changes with which accounting information can, without assuming a subjective point of view, be concerned.

Returning to more familiar ground in order to set up a relationship between the business decision-making process and information, note that individual decision-makers face various degrees of uncertainty in the various decision-making activities. For some decisions, they are almost certain as to what they should do. In such a situation, an item of news confirming a condition about which the decision-maker was almost certain would not provide a great deal of help to him. Such a bit of news would represent a small amount of information because it would not reduce significantly the decision-maker's condition of uncertainty. Recall, however, that the amount of information is quite distinct from the value of information, because the value of information typically refers to the income or utility increase resulting from the use of the information. The distinction between amount and value of information is best revealed by an example. Thus, if a decision-maker were fairly certain that he should decide to take action A rather than action B, a news item confirming that he should decide on A would represent a small amount of information. But, if the income difference between action A and action B were $50,000, the small amount of information could be of considerable value. The point is that the value of information depends upon the decision-making opportunities available to the decision-maker and not on his uncertainty about them. On the average, or over the long run, assuming income opportunities are random in nature, there would be a high correlation between the amount and value of information. In the macro sense of this study, they may, therefore, be considered as similar measures. To avoid any misunderstanding, however, this study is confined to the relationship of the amount of information to the business decision-making process. With this relationship between the amount and value of information in mind, recall that if a decision-maker were highly uncertain as to which among possible alternative decisions he should select, a news item indicating the proper decision to make would be of considerable help to him and would represent a large amount of information, unless a certain psychological point, which will be examined in a few moments, has been reached.

The relationship of business decision-making uncertainty to information is best examined with the diagram on the following page.

In order to simplify comprehension of the diagram, the explanation will start with a discussion of the curves in the first quadrant. Presumably, this is the condition of the business world today, although one has doubts at times that there really is more information than misinformation now provided business decision-makers.

Briefly, the curves in the first quadrant reveal that, as environmental complexity goes from low to high, the decision-maker's uncertainty condition, his entropy, increases at a rapid rate. This is reflected in the "uncertainty-level" curve. The function of information appears on the chart as one of reducing the amount of uncertainty from the total area between the uncertainty-level curve and the positive x-axis to the cross-hatched portion between the uncertainty-level curve and the "amount of information" curve. The curves indicate that the gap between the uncertainty level and the amount of information gradually increases as the uncertainty-level curve increases at a rapid rate; whereas the amount of information curve decreases at a rather rapid rate until, from point 2 on, increases in data actually decrease the amount of information provided decision-makers.

The curves in the first quadrant appear intuitively reasonable. The idea that an increase in the number of variables, conditions, or events to be considered a part of the environment causes decision-making uncertainty to rise tends to agree with one's personal experience when confronted with too many factors to be considered in making a decision. Also, the idea that information helps reduce uncertainty, until one gets so much of it that it cannot be comprehended, agrees with one's personal psychological experience. The curves are based on more than intuition, however, for they are supported in general by certain research studies in psychology.[1] Limited direct confirmation of their validity at the micro level has been provided by a nonquantitative empirical research study of the reactions of a purchasing agent of a university. In this research, the purchasing agent's area of purchasing responsibilities was increased substantially. This resulted in, and

1. See unpublished study by Professor Lawrence S. Revsine, University of Illinois (Urbana-Champaign, Illinois).

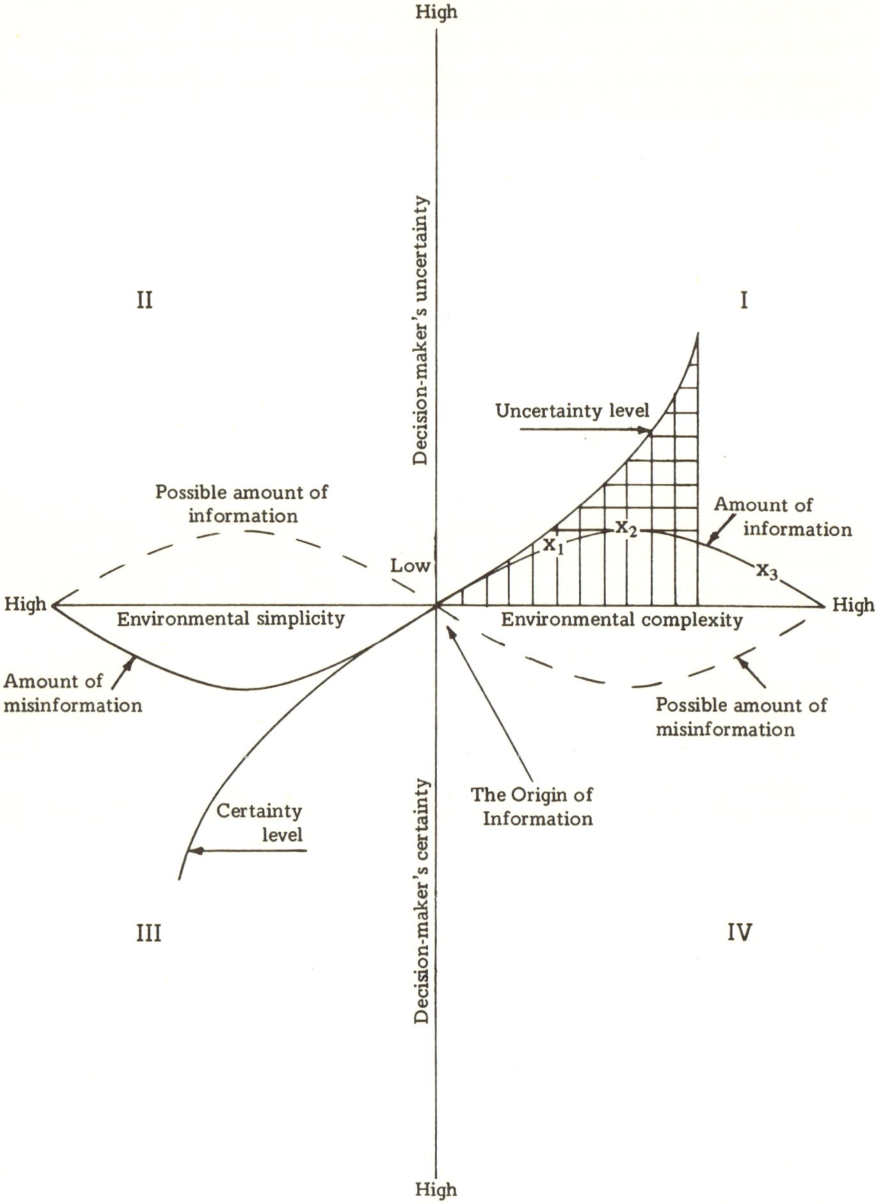

Relationship of Business Decision-Making Uncertainty to Information

was treated as, an increase in environmental complexity. The additional responsibilities were assigned as though they were new permanent responsibilities. Under the research project, this condition prevailed for one month. At the same time, using a computer, the amount of data pertinent to the decisions to be made was increased to the point that the purchasing agent could not read it all. At the end of the month, confusion reigned supreme. Although further research on the validity of the curves is needed for purposes of developing a sensitivity to the interrelationships among information, business, and society, the curves have been accepted as valid in this analysis.

The agonizing part about the curves in the first quadrant is that as a society we do not know where, at the macro level, business decision-making uncertainty and information now exist on the curve. It is a question of considerable concern to accountants whether business is now supplied data at level 1, 2, or 3. The fact that many business executives have employees digest and brief information reports suggests that our business-information condition may be beyond point 2. Other requests for information from business executives suggest that the present condition may be closer to point 1 than to point 2. On balance, considering the twentyfold increase in paper work in business in the last fifteen years, one is inclined to the view that, overall, the present business information condition may be on the downward slope of the information curve. Supporting this view is the statement of a scientist at Arthur D. Little that in the seventies, one of the three major problems facing business and society will be "a surfeit of information" that may engulf us all before we can do anything about the other two problems—pollution and a lack of energy sources. On the other hand, the rather amazing success of business as reflected in the growth of the gross national product implies that some very sound business decisions have been made in recent years. This, in turn, implies that the environmental complexity is not so involved that decision-making must take place under conditions of high uncertainty. In this context, one is inclined to the view that the prevailing uncertainty level has not reached excessive heights and may be somewhere near a point on the uncertainty-level curve directly vertical from point 2 on the information curve.

The determination of the present point on the two curves is a critical problem for accountants. If, for example, empirical research supports the belief that too many data are now being provided decision-makers, it means that accountants will have to redirect research toward means for compressing information (possibly along the lines Baruch Lev suggested in his research study on information theory and accounting) and toward means for improving the accounting perception process in order to be more selective in recognizing data for processing. Broadly, the implication is that accounting research ought to be directed toward compression and selectivity methods.

With the explanation of the first quadrant curves complete, it is relatively easy to grasp the meaning of the curves in the third quadrant. As "environmental simplicity" increases along the x-axis, the "certainty level" in which decisions are made increases more than proportionately. Mitigating against the implication that the source of peace and contentment of man is withdrawal from the hostility of the presently perceived environment is the emergence of misinformation in society. From misinformation arises (1) distrust among men due to lack of communication; (2) myths and false guides for action, due to lack of knowledge, as studies of certain tribes of Africa reveal; and (3) general confusion among men regarding proper action. Ultimately, excessive misinformation will be categorized as irrelevant and ignored for decision-making, and the amount of misinformation curve will turn up toward the x-axis. While this situation is not relevant to the topic of this paper, for conceptual completeness one might conclude that movement to the left on the environmental simplicity x-axis, while tending to create a condition of certainty in decision-making, really represents a return to animallike life, where decisions are made on the basis of instinct and intuition.

The second quadrant curve indicates that, if information is increased as the environment becomes more simple, the amount of certainty in decision-making increases. This is reflected in the area between the "possible amount of information" curve in the second quadrant and the certainty-level curve in the third quadrant.

It is in the fourth quadrant that the role of misinformation in modern society is revealed. Essentially, increases in incorrect data increase, up to a point, the decision-making uncertainty area lying between the uncertainty-level curve in the first quadrant and the "possible amount of misinformation" curve in the fourth quadrant. While empirical evidence on the role of misinformation in modern society is lacking, limited analyses and intuitive reactions indicate that at least two types of misinformation prevail in modern society:

(1) purposely released misinformation, in the form of propaganda intended to widen the decision-making uncertainty area until confu-

sion results and man is no longer able to act in his best interest; and

(2) nonpurposely released information, in the form of inadequate perception by message receivers and inadequate sensing of the environment.

The implication of the curve in the fourth quarter is that, while misleading advertising pays, if the objective is to confuse the decision-making of others, it pays only up to a point. One might, in an optimistic mood, suggest that the curve implies that if we get enough misinformation in society people might ultimately tend to ignore it and use only reliable information. This possibility has implications for the auditing function in society, for audited information would be reliable information. Of course, to the extent that the auditing function becomes more fully recognized as one of providing reliable information, there will have to occur a significant expansion in both the auditing tools and technology and the scope of applications of the auditing function in society. There is, in fact, some evidence to indicate that auditing has taken a few first steps along the long road of developing reliable information for society.

As to where our society now stands on the possible amount of misinformation curve in the fourth quadrant, one can only hope that we are near the nadir and that the depth of the misinformation curve is not so much greater than the height of the information curve that misinformation's devisive role is on the wane in modern society. As of now, man can only make his guesses and call for extensive social psychology research.

Returning to the main topic of this paper, note that there is a subtle intuitive implication reflected in the first quadrant curves to the effect that the "environmental complexity" of business is constantly increasing in American society and is creating a more than proportionate increase in the entropy facing business decision-makers. What is the evidence to support such a proposition? Actually, there is precious little, and the problem becomes one of searching for evidence. Broadly, there appear to be two reasonable ways to look for this evidence. One is to examine developments in the business world itself; the other is to examine the problem of the business environment from the point of view of society.

As to the developments in the business world itself, it seems most convincing to note a few specific environmental developments since World War II which reveal that business decision-makers face a constantly increasing complex business environment. For example:

(1) There has been an increasing specialization of workers, which has created much greater interdependence among business actions. As a result of the increasing interdependence, the business decision-maker has become well aware that the consequences of a decision may be felt in many other parts of the business world. Reactions to decisions come from unexpected places.

(2) The size of large business entities has increased significantly, which creates the possibility that a lower-level decision-maker may be suboptimizing his own area of responsibility to the detriment of other areas of the total entity. This would be so because of his inability to grasp and relate all activities of the total entity.

(3) The population explosion has been widely recognized and, because it increases more than proportionately the communication channels which could exist among people, makes decision-makers aware of the difficulty of their task of discerning changes in the wants and needs of society which have to be satisfied by business.

(4) The knowledge explosion since World War II has created multiple ways of doing things. Products can be produced and distributed in different ways and the correct way at one particular point in time depends upon the circumstances. Overall, the result is a more complex environment for decision-making.

(5) Organizations have become more complex in a psychological sense. That is, involved motivational and inspirational devices are used to coordinate effective employee relationships. These devices are part of the business environment as tools which the decision-maker must consider using in selecting courses of action.

These five situations are illustrative and not conclusive evidence that the business environment seems to be becoming more and more complex. It is hoped, however, that the illustrations are sufficient to generate support for the proposition that the business environment is now most complex and that business itself is a highly interdependent structure of separate entities. The illustrations do not reveal trends, let alone a rate of trend change; thus, they afford no basis for predicting the future, except possibly to imply that things will be different. Yet, if one aspires to establish a set of relationships among information, business, and society, it would be highly desirable to be able to predict developments in one of these areas and then to use the developed relationships to predict developments in other areas. An examination of the cause of changes in the business world is therefore appropriate.

It is assumed to be impossible to even recognize, let alone itemize and categorize, all the forces for change in the business world. But a study of a number of them suggests that technology underlies them all. The proposition accepted in this study is that technology is the most powerful force for change in the business environment and that its influence seems to be increasing. At the macro level, this suggests that, if means were available to forecast technological change, that forecast could be used to predict the future complexity of the business decision-maker's environment.

Technological forecasting is a relatively new discipline. Its methodology is not well developed, but some of its current findings are significant to anyone interested in the information needs of future society. Some of these are discussed in the following pages. The first finding of significance is that applications of technological forecasting proceed as shown in the accompanying diagram.

The elongated S curve is based on a number of empirical studies which indicate that business use of technological development proceeds through a pioneering stage at a slow rate of application then accelerates until new applications are rapidly introduced. This stage of rapid applications continues until the possibilities of application tend toward exhaustion at the upper level of the curve.

The expectation line is the significant line to accountants. This line reflects the human tendency to extrapolate linearly, and the gap between the "expectation line" and the "application line" represents an information gap in society which needs to be corrected and for which accountants might assume a responsibility. The gap when expectations lag behind actual applications, area A on the graph, is serious in that it develops an indifferent attitude on the part of decision-makers that tends to foster careless decision-making and a disdain for advanced decision-making technology. It needs to be corrected by an improved information system if business decision-making is to be performed in harmony with environmental developments. It is the gap in area B on the graph that is much more significant, however, for, when expectations exceed realization, human frustration and conflict result, which, in turn, tend to result in an undesirable atmosphere that can only do harm for the institution of business. While the implication of the following graph on the application of one technological development may be quite significant to decision-makers in an industry devoted to its development, for all of business, interest attaches to the rate at which new technological developments are introduced into society. The limited evidence available suggests that in an overall sense the rate of technological innovation is still in a period of rapid expansion. As fast as one technological development is exploited and fully applied, new developments occur, so that, in the envelope-curve context, the rate of total technological change in society is rapidly upward and may even be accelerating.

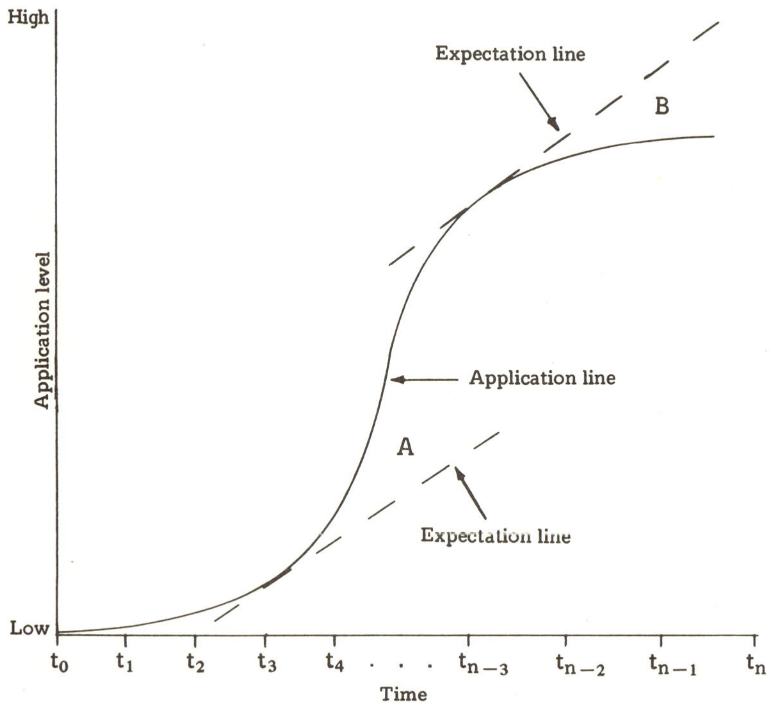

Extent of Utilization of Technological Development

The fact is that, up until 1800, technological activity was under the control of an authoritarian philosophy of life. Authoritative pronouncements were accepted without question and without testing them against reality. Starting before but emerging as a replacement to the authoritarian philosophy of life about 1800 came the philosophy of "experimentally tested thought," widely heralded as the scientific method. This method of experimentally tested thought generated a steady acceleration of technological development which carried over into an expanded role for business in society. But the limitation to the tested thought philosophy is that different specialized fields of study were kept quite distinct, and this separateness of fields of study resulted in duplicate and redundant basic work in different fields. Because the fields were not coordinated, technological advances did not occur as rapidly as they might have. Moving now in the waning years of the twentieth century to complement the philosophy of experimentally tested thought is the philosophy of "interfield innovation" to motivate and control human and technological developments. The central goal of this new emerging philosophy of life is to "satisfy human needs"; it is reflected in newspaper jargon as "the cult of the young," "the student revolt," or "the hippie movement." Actually, the only reason the new philosophy is mislabeled as a youth movement is that many post-thirty members of society, having attained some degree of security in society, have lost the sharpness of their sensitivity to new developments. But whatever its cause and precise nature, the new philosophy of interfield innovation breaks down the barriers among different fields of study and provides for the use, under an overall systems approach, of developments in any field that promises to further a technological advance. The result of this mingling of various fields of study reduces duplicate studies, broadens perspective, and tends to accelerate even more technological advances in all parts of society. Now, as this occurs, the dependence of business decision-makers on formal information will increase rapidly. This is so, because past experience is not repeated in a time of such rapid change and the information informally obtained by decision-makers by experience over the years past loses its relevance. The implication is that so rigid is to be the relationship between business and information in the future that business decision-making may become an information function, with the power of business flowing to the centers of information.

The conclusion that technological change is to increase at an increasing rate is supported by a number of technological forecasts in such diverse areas as (1) the speed of aircraft; (2) human transportation speeds, in general, which suggest, incidentally, that by the year 2350 we shall be approaching the speed of light; (3) efficiency of fuel-burning electric power plants; (4) rate of improvement in the grinding process; (5) efficiency of illumination sources; (6) lowest temperature achieved in the laboratory by artificial means; (7) machine tool tolerances; (8) micro-engineering; and (9) installed technological horsepower in the United States. Illustrative of the results of these

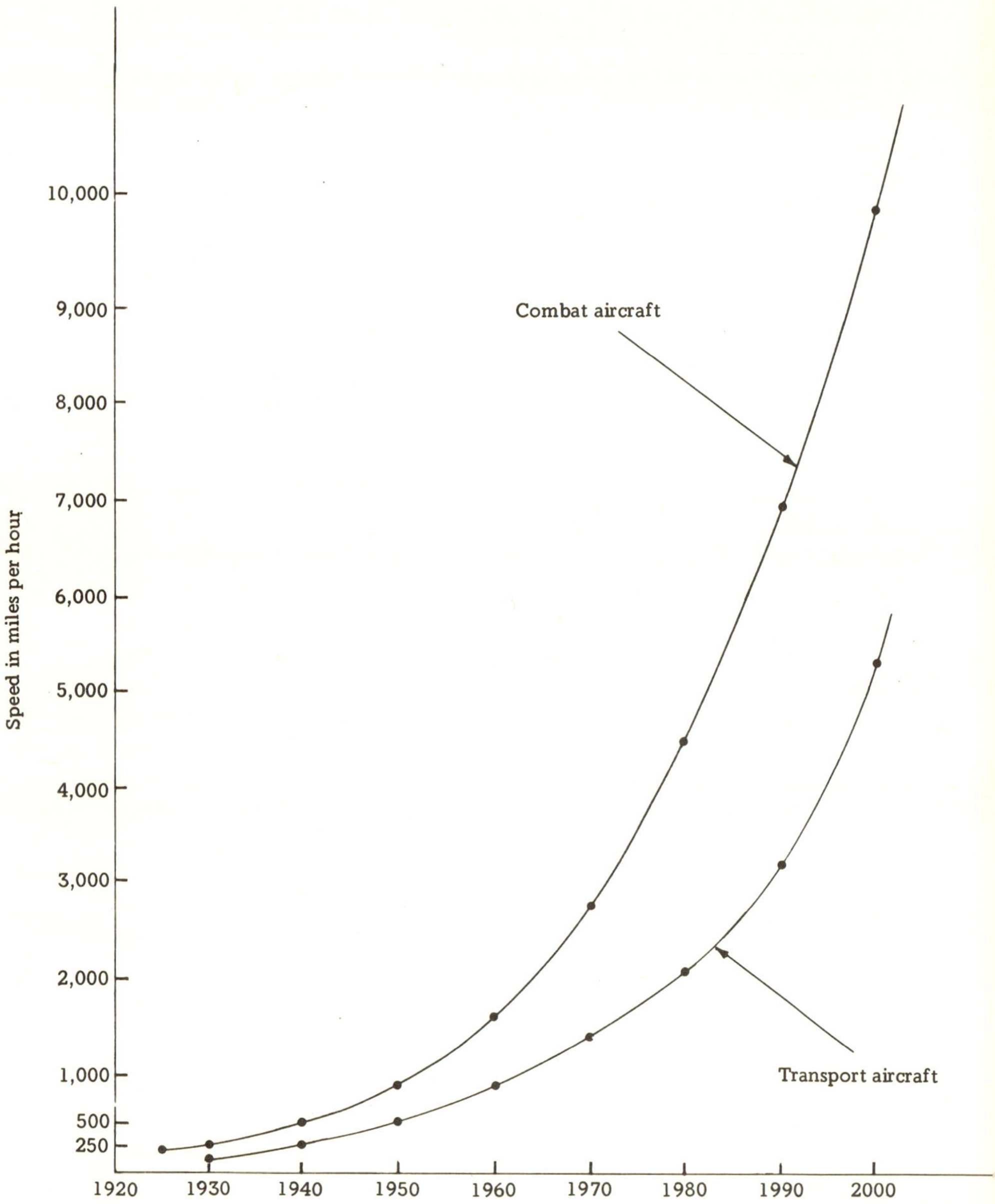

Trend of Aircraft Speed

technological forecasts is the accompanying chart of maximum aircraft speed for the period 1925 to 2000.[2]

The implication so far is that information and business are going to be much more interrelated in the future than in the past. There has also been an implication, based on the premise that the main force for change in business is technology, that the business environment of the future is going to change rapidly and will need a greatly improved *quality* of information in the future. This emerging problem of information quality, with which accountants are becoming increasingly concerned, is viewed as the solution to the previously discussed possibility that excessive data, posing as information, are now being presented to business decision-makers. The conclusion is that accounting research of the future ought to be directed primarily to the two problems of:

(1) developing a methodology for compressing information; and

(2) developing perception processes to improve the selectivity of information.

It would be of interest to make a prediction of the probability that the information-development process of the future, still known as accounting presumably, will be adequate to supply the information needs of the future. Unfortunately, this symposium came about six months too soon to include actual data into the information-prediction model which I believe appropriate for this question. The model, adapted from a study by A. L. Floyd of Lockheed Aircraft, is based on the trend of the "amount of information per bit of data communicated." The forecast is to be based on the calculation of a probability of improving the information per data bit through applied research effort. The model appears somewhat as follows.

The probability that a researcher will improve the quality of information (quantity of information per data bit) on one research project from level 1 to level 2 would be:

$$(1) \quad P(2,1) = \frac{X}{M}, \text{ where:}$$

X is the number of possible research projects that would result in an advance in the information per data bit from level 1 to level 2; and M is the total number of research projects that could be undertaken by the researcher.

2. Adapted from James R. Bright, ed., *Technological Forecasting for Industry and Government* (Englewood Cliffs, N.J.: Prentice-Hall, 1968), p. 68.

If this basic formula (1) is expanded to include the average number of qualified researchers $\bar{R}$, each completing $\bar{N}$ research projects per period of time, the probability that the accounting profession will advance the information per data bit to a given level L in a given time span (Δt) would be:

$$(2)\quad P(L,\Delta t) = 1 - \left(1 - \frac{X}{M}\right)^{\bar{N}\bar{R}(\Delta t)}$$

This states that the probability of advancing the quality of accounting information to level L is merely 1 minus the probability of not advancing to the new level.

Practically, it is believed that a measure of both $\frac{X}{M}$ and I (information per data bit) can be simulated by a research project on this issue using accounting reports over the period 1933–1970. These initial measures of the ratio of successful research projects to projects attempted and of the information per data bit at level 1 can be used as a starting point. It is assumed that the information per data bit can be improved—by any one of a number of itemized possible research projects. The itemization of possible research projects is still an open-ended project in itself that will be arbitrarily closed on August 31, 1970, after approximately two hours' study per week for one year.

Now, given the objective of improving the quality of information per data bit and the finite number of possible research projects M of which X will result in an improvement in the information per data bit, it is evident that as improvements are made in I (information per data bit), the number of successful research projects remaining to be completed will decrease slightly. However, if one posits a limit to the information per data bit of I = 50 per cent of the uncertainty condition, it is apparent that as the level of I approaches this limit due to research results, the number of remaining successful research projects must approach 0.

For purposes of this model under development, it will be assumed that the rate of change in the remaining successful research projects is proportional to the number of research projects used to develop the quality of information to the prevailing higher level above level 1. This may be expressed as:

$$(3)\quad \frac{\Delta X}{\Delta 2} = -k(M - X), \text{ where:}$$

$\Delta 2$ is the change in the level of I; and
k is a constant.

Integrating equation (3) between the level 2 amount of information per data bit and the limiting value of I, defined as E, while X ranges from 0 to X, $\frac{X}{M}$ is found as follows:

$$(4)\quad \frac{X}{M} = \int_{X}^{0} \frac{dx}{M - X} = -k \int_{2}^{E} d2,$$

which may be expressed as:

$$\frac{X}{M} = 1 - \exp\left[-k(E - 2)\right].$$

Note that equation (4) does not recognize that X and M change with time and that k could be time-dependent.

Now, if we substitute the derived value $\frac{X}{M}$ into equation (2), we have:

$$(5)\quad P(L,\Delta t) = 1 - \exp\left[-(E - 2)k\bar{N}\bar{R}(\Delta t)\right].$$

This means that the probability of moving the quality of information per data bit I to level 1 over any period of time is equal to the difference between $1 - \bar{P}(t)$ and the result of multiplying the probabilities of not achieving level L as follows:

$$(6)\quad P(L,t) = 1 - \exp\left[-(E - 2) \int_{00}^{t} k\bar{N}\bar{R}(\Delta t)\right].$$

Now the trouble with equation (6) is that, although it replaces the sum of all the $k\bar{N}\bar{R}(\Delta t)$ elements in equation (5) with the integral, the integral cannot be evaluated because the number of researchers R can be varied, which significantly influences the rate of time by which the quality of information is improved.

But is it possible to assume that, once the accounting profession shifts its interest to the improvement of the quality of their information and away from the quantity of data, researchers will shift from efforts to develop additional data bits to the new area of research. While the form of this shift in interest is not known, it is assumed that the rate of shift is a function of the difference in the amount of information provided by improving the quality of information over increasing the quantity of information in the same period of time. Then the number of researchers available to carry out research projects to improve the quality of information could be estimated as:

$$(7) \quad R = R(f_{ge} - f_{gn})R_o(t), \text{ where:}$$

f_{ge} = effectiveness measure of improving accounting information by improving quality;
f_{gn} = effectiveness measure of improving accounting information by increasing quantity; and
$R_o(t)$ = the growth rate of total accounting researchers.
Then, the first order approximation $(f_{ge} - f_{gn})$ can be used to make the assumption that:

$$(8) \quad R = (f_{ge} - f_{gn})R_o(t).$$

Now assuming that k and N in equation (6) are relatively constant, equation (8) can be placed in equation (6) to yield:

$$(9) \quad P(L,t) = 1 - \exp\left[-(E-2)\int_{00}^{t}(f_{ge} - f_{gn})T(t)dt\right], \text{ where:}$$

T(t) is a function which varies with time and is equal to

$$k(t) \cdot \bar{N}(t) \cdot R_o(t).$$

For future projections, the probability P(L,t) may be held at a constant 50 percent value, and then the way the information per data bit improves with time can be estimated. By setting P(L,t) = .5, the integral in equation (9) can be evaluated by separation of variables with the result that:

$$(10) \quad P(L,t) = .5 = 1 - \exp\left[\frac{-.6931\,(C_1t + C_2)}{Y + \ln(Y-1) + C_2}\right], \text{ where:}$$

$Y = \dfrac{1 - f_{gn}/E}{1 - f_{ge}/E}$;
C_1, C_2 are constants; and
the integral of T(t) = constant times change in time for the finite ranges of time considered.

Equation (10) is the basis for plotting and projecting the trend of changes in the quality of information (information per data bit). Three measurements are necessary to use it:

(1) the limit of the information per data bit to which we aspire;

(2) the extent to which accounting information can be improved by increasing quantity must be estimated; and

(3) the value of C_1 must be determined from at least two data points.

Lacking data to test the formula at this time but putting it through the computer with arbitrary numbers and comparing it with the trend of technological changes as exemplified on page 14 as a reflection of the change in business environment, one develops an apprehension that accounting information, including that developed by management science technology, cannot be developed rapidly enough to be adequate for the needs of business decision-makers well before the year 2000.

Turning now to an examination of environmental complexity from the point of view of society as a whole, it seems appropriate to confine the concept of environment to the set of human activities and those parts of the physical environment to which there is a human reaction. This set of human activities is, from a broad structural sociological point of view, merely the interactions among individuals or groups in society. These interactions are governed by the socially accepted modes of thought and action of individuals or groups. In addition to these social norms, which stimulate specific actions by individuals and groups, cultural values indicate in general how a group or an individual in a society will behave. For example, in some societies the majority of the population may prefer football. In other societies the majority may prefer opera. The interrelated mass of these norms and values represents the framework or structure of society in the sense that the mass is all tied together in a sort of interconnected network of relationships. The status and functioning of this unified, total human social structure imposes realistic restraints on the activities or operations of individual business firms within that society. Illustrative of these restraints are such business commandments as:

(1) Business action shall not disturb the social norms of private property and freedom of choice.

(2) Business action shall not disturb suddenly the cultural values which provide stability to a society.

(3) Business actions shall not disturb those aspects of the physical environment which influence social norms and cultural values.

Subject to a multitude of manifest and latent social and physical constraints such as those listed, business seems to have relatively free choice in what it chooses to do. There is, however, a growing realization in the business world today that the chosen objective of optimizing the economic operations of the business entity may have so dominated business interests that both the established social norms and cultural values of American society have been weakened, with the result that total human society seems, to many members of society, to be falling apart. As evidence, they point not only to the pollution of our physical environment but also to the apparent loss of purpose in human life emerging in our total society. It is this disorganization of the human environment and its tendency to destroy meaning in life, they contend, that represents the present-day environment with which business decision-makers must be concerned in planning (budgeting) and controlling the operation of a business entity.

In more precise terms, it seems that the impact of the excessive interest in economic objectives, along with a multiple list of other factors such as the population increase, industrialization, and higher education, seem to have, according to the economic law of diminishing utility, dulled human sensitivity to social norms and cultural values to such an extent that a decrease in the stability of human responses to specific stimuli is in reality what has occurred. As a result, it becomes more and more difficult to predict behavior, and, to the casual observer, society does indeed seem to be falling apart. This instability of the human response increases with rapid changes. The overall result is an increase in the uncertainty condition on the part of the people who must act, which manifests itself in an increased risk to business operations and even to the business institution itself. These risks, it must be reiterated, are due to the instability of the human response to the traditional stimuli of values and norms. They are now environmental constraints of such magnitude that they must be considered in business operations and budgeting; whereas, they may have been recognized informally in the past when they were less significant elements.

The point being made is that business must adjust its activities to be in accord with the prevailing cultural values and norms of the society in which it operates. This relationship between business and society is becoming more and more a rigid relationship that cannot be violated. Furthermore, it is the function of information to enable business to comply with this relationship. In an effort to restrict the scope of this paper, the opposite problem of the set of responsibilities of society to business is not considered.

With this background in mind, it is time to discuss the nature of society and the way it is changing toward the objective of determining more precisely the relationships among information, business, and society that will prevail in the future.

As to the nature of the components (the specific elements of the social environment) which should be considered in providing information for business planning and budgeting and to managers for operating business entities, there seem to be as many views as there are social scientists. The problem is an ever present consideration, however, for all societies in human history have had to operate according to the restrictions of the relationships among the values and norms of society. But the situation is more acute today, for not only is the world most complex, but it is also highly interrelated and this interrelatedness means that actions in one part of a complex society may have an unknown impact in another part of society. It is, therefore, particularly important that business firms view and understand the whole system of human society before they seek to improve the operations of their subpart of that whole system. Otherwise, they may do more harm than good to the total system. It may well be that the cause of much of the unfavorable view of business today is the tendency of business entities to suboptimize their own entity operations to the detriment of the whole human social system. It may be fair to contend that the failure of business decision-makers to consider the constraints imposed by society on business operations and budgeting has caused business firms to fail to respond to the changed social system arising in the post-World War II period. It may be that business has not clearly perceived its role in society. It may be that business in general has not recognized that the interests and values of society have to be part of the interests and values of the business, because business is merely part of society. It seems reasonable to suggest that businessmen must quit thinking about their "social responsibilities," because the term implies that business is separated from society. Rather, business has to start thinking about the role of business in society and to consider the proper functions of business in human society. Business must stop thinking that the subparts of society (and business is merely one of many subparts) are relatively independent of the whole system. Businessmen must operate and budget in terms of the whole society system.

It is the overwhelming task of information to see that business is sufficiently informed to make this adjustment, and accountants must begin to so think. This requirement—that businessmen must think in terms of the whole social environment—is a requirement that will be extremely difficult for accountants to implement. It has been pointed out previously that technological change alone is going to increase the complexity of business operations to such an extent that a doubt arose that information developers could meet that need by the year 2000. Now, consideration of the social environment and the realization that business must be more sensitive to and more cooperative with that social environment places an even greater burden on the information function in society.

The only reasonable approach to this aspect of the functioning of accounting information and business appears to be to assume that the social environment faced by business decision-makers can be understood by studying the manifest and latent communications network prevailing in total society. The type of communication network referred to is the flow of all types of messages throughout the environment, where the term "message" is used in its broad sense as the transmission of motivational stimuli that cause action. If the business entity were well wired into this total communication network by an expanded monitoring information system, it could become aware of the constraints which the environment is placing on its operations. It seems reasonable to suggest that it is the responsibility of accounting information, as one likes to view accounting, to see that business starts becoming well wired, by an information network, into all activities of society, in order that society will continue to accept the institution of business as we know it. Limited historical evidence indicates that society measures organizational goals in terms of their perceived contribution to the functioning of the total system of which the single organization is only a part. Organizational business goals become an operational subset of the aims of the society and must be devised, interpreted, and implemented within that essential social environmental constraint. Not to do so ensures the failure not only of the individual business manager but of the institution of business as well. Thus, the goal-setting problem of an organization includes the task of determining a relationship of the organization to the larger society.

The set of relationships between business and society must be such that it will be apparent that the question of what business organization goals shall be depends significantly upon what society wants done or can be persuaded by business to support. Furthermore, since changes in both business organizations and society are constantly taking place and will alter organization goals, these goals need to be constantly reviewed and altered appropriately. As further explanation of the nature of the set of relationships between business and society, note that the goals of a business organization determine the kind of goods and services which the organization will produce and offer to society. When the goals are easily identified, social appraisal and evaluation of goals may be accomplished by referring to appropriate accounting data. When goals are intangible and not clearly evident to society, the social appraisal of the goals and the effectiveness with which they are carried out is much more difficult; social unrest arises. This means that information must facilitate public awareness of the extent to which business goals are in harmony with the goals of total society. Presumably, this could be accomplished by an expansion of the auditing concept in society.

In conclusion, some consideration must be given to the problem of predicting the future values and norms of society in order to attempt to arrange a set of relationships among information, business, and society that will span time and further the development of civilization.[3]

Although the notion of a norm or value change is readily understood at a very general level of consideration, the forecasting of specific norm or value changes is most involved. There are great complexities in the way different ones interact with one another.

Note first that a norm-value change is generally not a matter of subscribing to or abandoning a certain norm or value. Rather, it is a matter of the extent to which the norm-value is believed and the way it is grouped with others. Also, the norm-values of society tend to conflict with one another when taken in the aggregate in just the way our life-needs (for rest, amusement, exercise, and rewarding activity) contradict one another in competing for time, attention, and resources.

The practical importance of the problem of future norm-values is so great, however, that attempts to deal with it cannot be abandoned because of its difficulties. With this reservation constantly in mind, the subsequent considerations of future American norm-values will consider those values itemized by the working party on "values and rights" of the Commission on the Year 2000 of the American Academy of Arts and Sciences. In the deliberations of this commission, the following norm-values were regarded as particularly affected by or involved in foreseeable future developments:

(1) Privacy

3. Much of the following material on value change was obtained from a lecture by Professor Nicholas Rescher at the University of Texas in 1969.

(2) Equality (legal, social, and economic)
(3) Personal integrity (versus depersonalization)
(4) Welfare (personal and social)
(5) Freedom (of choice and action)
(6) Law abidingness and public order
(7) Pleasantness of environment
(8) Social adjustment
(9) Efficiency and effectiveness in organizations
(10) Rationality (organizational and individual)
(11) Education and intelligence
(12) Ability and talent.

Actually, the values in this list can be sorted into three categories as follows:

(1) *Individual rights norm-values*—privacy, equality, personal integrity, welfare, freedom

(2) *Life-setting norm-values*—public order, pleasantness of environment

(3) *Personal characteristic norm-values*—efficiency, rationality, social adjustment, education, intelligence, ability, talent.

Each of the norm-values in the basic list can also be placed into one of the two categories as (1) threatened in the future, or (2) needed in the future. Individual rights norm-values and life-setting norm-values clearly fall into the threatened category in that their realization is apt to be substantially more difficult in the future society. The condition of being needed appears to be the lot of the personal characteristic norm-values in that their espousal, maintenance, and realization will be especially important in the future society.

In addition to the basic list of social and ability norm-values, there can be little question that the character norm-values of honesty, loyalty, idealism, friendliness, and truthfulness will have a yet greater need in the crowded, depersonalized, and complex society of the future, however highly these values may have been prized heretofore. American society has treasured these character values throughout its history, but in the future they will very likely be markedly upgraded as a social environment takes shape in which they are increasingly indispensable. Witness the call of the youth for honesty in government. The plain fact is that over the past generation there has been a marked tendency in American norm-values to shift from the notion of "getting ahead in the world" to the notion of "service to mankind." This is a trend that will certainly continue and possibly intensify.

Although there is no quantified basis for the projection, the forecast is that known changes in specific values are underway and that business must adjust to them. Accountants should aspire to provide the information to enable the adjustments to be made.

Overall, the responsibility of the information function in discovering, developing, and maintaining a desirable set of relationships between business and society is an appalling comprehension. When one realizes that society is not a static structure and that there is a need for a constant awareness of the changes taking place in society, it seems quite clear that American society is going to have to direct a much greater portion of its resources to the information industry. It seems that accountants ought now to be doing research on methods for perceiving and monitoring both internal and external activities in and surrounding business and that they should be attempting to develop new concepts of significance and of objectivity.

Discussion on Norton Bedford Paper "Information, Business, and Society"

John T. Wheeler

WHEN I AGREED to be the discussant for the Bedford paper, I did not realize I would be expected to comment on information, business, and society, and all in fifteen minutes. Professor Bedford has treated us to a tour de force of accounting as the information system of business in the society of the seventies. I could not possibly comment on all facets of his presentation. Instead, I would like to focus on three issues raised in the paper which I believe are of utmost importance to accountants, the future of accounting, and the foundations of accounting theory.

First, the relationship between information systems and accounting needs to be explored. Some people view the two as almost synonymous. Others look at a subsystem of information called the management-information system and equate it with accounting. This is the position which Bedford seems to take. For example, he states, "It seems reasonable to suggest that it is the responsibility of accounting information, as one likes to view accounting, to see that business starts becoming well wired, by an information network, into all activities of society, in order that society will continue to accept the institution of business as we know it."

I take a much more limited view of accounting as a special form of an information system limited to data expressed in monetary terms and with a generally agreed upon set of rules for the collection, manipulation, and dissemination of data for the use of decision-makers. I have the old-fashioned notion that the people in market research, production control, personnel, public relations, etc., have a role to play in the total management-information system.

The present trend of accountants is in the direction attributed to philosophers who learn less and less about more and more until they know nothing about everything. We know little enough now without compounding our ignorance by trying to encompass within accounting all aspects of information or even of management information. There is nothing in the training, experience, or personal characteristics of accountants to indicate a competence for providing information to business decision-makers concerning changes in legal, social, and political factors in the environment within which business operates or concerning changes in human factors within the organization. Accountants need to define clearly the area within which they will operate and be certain that they possess the competence to perform at a high level within the scope of their defined activities.

Second, the relationship between accounting and our business system needs to be clarified. There is a distinct symbiotic relationship between accounting and business. Business could not have developed to its present complexity without the related advancements in accounting, and accounting has been forced to grow in stature to retain its place in business and provide its segment of information to management, investors, government, and the general public. Accounting, however, is not the handmaiden of business, and it is not the role of accountants to preserve any particular institutions or specific economic system. Accounting is a universal type of information system which is needed in every known form of economic system and by all resource-using people or organizations within those systems. In our own society, accounting is as vital to government as to business, to nonprofit organizations as to business firms. We need to expand our horizons but not so much in terms of a larger role within the business firm but rather to a larger role within society by giving more attention to our possible service to nonbusiness organizations and to society in general.

This does not mean that the role of accounting in business cannot grow or should not change. Accounting is an indispensable element in the operation of business in a free-enterprise economy. If one studies the more limited role which accounting plays in firms in centrally planned socialist economies, it becomes evident that, despite the many limitations in the present state of accounting, the operation of complex industrial organizations in an increasingly complex society has been made possible by the sophisticated information role of modern accounting.

I find myself in rather strong disagreement with Bedford on the role of individual business firms within our society. He states, "The status and functioning of this unified, total human social structure imposes realistic restraints on the activities or operations of individual business firms within that society. Illustrative of these restraints are such business commandments as: (1) Business action shall not disturb the social norms of private property and freedom of choice. [I believe business should operate so as to demonstrate that these are viable social norms in our emerging society.] (2) Business action shall not disturb suddenly the cultural values which provide stability to a society. [This places business in a conservative role, but business was once a revolutionary force in society, and it needs to return to this position if it is to provide leadership in bringing about a new and better society.] (3) Business actions shall not disturb those aspects of the physical environment which influence social norms and cultural values. [Business must disturb the physical environment, but it should do so in a way which will contribute positively to the determination and attainment of social norms and cultural values.]"

In short, I would argue, as Bedford does, that business firms are merely a part of society and they must operate in conformance with the interests and values of society. This does not mean that business decision-makers should seek to preserve the status quo. Just as business has been an aggressive force in bringing about technological change, it should also operate so as to provide leadership in building a new and better society. Bedford speaks about interfield innovation with respect to technological change, but it is even more appropriate to apply this term to the essential role of business in bringing about change in general.

Third, the relationship between accounting and society needs to be developed. Accounting theory has developed with a theoretical foundation in the theory of the firm and the economic concept of business income. This strong tie to micro-economics has been of fundamental importance in the structure of accounting theory. We have, however, failed to develop a comparable foundation in macro-economics. Accounting should serve society, and the foundations of accounting theory should rest on welfare economics rather than on the theory of the business firm. Bedford has pointed to important forces in society which must be recognized by accountants, and, by implication at least, they should be factors in the emergence of new foundations for accounting theory. He states, "The proposition accepted in this study is that technology is the most powerful force for change in the business environment and that its influence seems to be increasing." He goes on to point out the emergence of the "philosophy of interfield innovation to motivate and control human and technological developments." He then explains that "the central goal of this new emerging philosophy of life is to 'satisfy human needs'; it is reflected in newspaper jargon as 'the cult of the young,' 'the student revolt,' or 'the hippie movement.' "

This view of technology appears to me to be outmoded. One of the messages of today is that the role of technology is to serve rather than determine. It is social values rather than technology which is the most powerful force for change in the business environment. Bedford, in a later section of his paper, seems to recognize this fact, and he emphasizes in particular how the rapidly changing society values increase environmental complexity and thus the need for information for the decision-maker. It is becoming increasingly evident that society is going to require technologists and business firms to turn their attention to solutions to problems which are of particular concern to society. Pollution, urban problems, population growth, and poverty are examples of issues which society wants to see solved even if this means diverting resources from other areas where the rate of technological advance might be more rapid such as space exploration.

Bedford emphasizes the role of business in interfield innovation, the importance of information to business, and thus the vital role of accounting in providing business with predictions of the "future values and norms of society in order to attempt to arrange a set of relationships among information, business, and society that will span time and further the development of civilization."

The implications of all of this for accounting research are pointed out by Bedford as follows: "The conclusion is that accounting research of the future ought to be directed primarily to the two problems of: (1) developing the methodology for compressing information; and (2) developing perception processes to improve the selectivity of information." In the original version of his paper which I received there was a misprint, so (2) read "Developing perception processes to improve the *seductivity* of information." I liked the original wording better, because there is something about the term "seductivity of information" which appeals to me. In either case, Bedford's prescription for future accounting research is good, but I do not find the needed prescription for the construction of the "foundations of accounting" theory.

I would summarize Bedford's message as encouragement for accounting to expand to provide the information needed by business to become well wired into all activities of society. That is, the emphasis is on society as the environment of business, business as a dynamic and integral force in a changing society, and accounting as a vital function in providing information for business decision-makers.

I would like to suggest a subtle but fundamental change in this picture. Accounting needs to expand to provide one vital type of information for all decision-makers in our changing society in order to facilitate the operations of all institutions of that society toward the attainment of the goal of the maximization of human welfare. Here, the emphasis is on accounting as one type of information system utilized by all segments of society in their quest for the good life for all mankind. If this approach is accepted, the conclusions follow that the foundations of accounting theory must rest on concepts of human welfare and that we should look to philosophy and welfare economics for useful concepts in its development. This is consistent with Bedford's emphasis on the macro approach, but it is more limited in scope. He refers at the beginning of his paper to the total systems approach, and this perspective is important, but it is my considered opinion that accounting must be viewed as a subsystem. Progress in the development of accounting theory will be dependent upon the careful definition of the scope and purpose of accounting and the total-information systems approach is antithetical to this objective.

Varieties of Accounting Theory

Louis Goldberg

William James has a sentence which may be pertinent to these discussions—but I hope it is not. "There is," he says, "a curious fascination in hearing deep things talked about, even though neither we nor the disputants understand them."[1]

Evidence of Confusion

The purpose of this paper is to try to distinguish between some of the senses in which the expression "accounting theory" has been and is being used, for there can be little doubt, surely, that it is used with different meanings and, indeed, with different objectives.

At first sight, it may seem that this is a very narrow purpose and merely an exercise in classification; to some extent it is, but I hope it will also lead to some clarification of ideas and perhaps some broadening, rather than narrowing, of our thinking about accounting.

The literature of accounting has not been especially notable for the precision of its terminology, and, if anybody doubts that there are discrepancies in usage of the expression mentioned, let him ponder just a few instances:

In the preface to his *Accounting Theory*, W. A. Paton made it clear

1. William James, *Pragmatism* (New York: Longmans Green, 1908), p. 5.

that he was expounding an entity theory of the accounting system to explain the recording and reporting processes of accounting as a counter to the then prevailing expository textbook presentation of the proprietary theory.[2] The premises and postulates explicitly listed in the final chapter of that classic work are for him assumptions which "accountants are sometimes in danger of forgetting"and which therefore indicate "limitations of their work."[3]

For A. C. Littleton, "accounting theory, since it has grown largely out of accounting practice, may seem to serve principally as a means of explaining and illuminating what is done in accounting. But theory has a further obligation, that of strengthening practice by subjecting customs to analysis and testing their justification by finding the relation of customary ideas to basic concepts and purposes."[4] Note here, incidentally, the personification of theory—it has obligations, it is able to do things, just as a human being. Among the many other observations of this author on accounting theory was this: "Theory can be an aid to understanding, and understanding united with practical wisdom can carry us a long way toward a good choice. Perhaps it is too much to expect either theory or practice to be completely satisfactory alone. I am convinced that theory could not, for theory does not direct; when we use theory we do not seek to prescribe. We are only trying to analyse, to understand, to persuade. Theory therefore must consist of explanations, definitions, reasons, justifications, persuasions. And only sometimes of suppositions and hypotheses."[5] He also states, "If we view the term broadly (that is, not confining it to 'a theory') theory can be properly called a body of doctrine. It is an area of beliefs, explanations, justifications, related to an area of practice. Its elements are descriptions, definitions, arguments, inferences, explanations, reasons—and principles."[6]

For Eldon S. Hendriksen, accounting theory is "logical reasoning in the form of a set of broad principles that (1) provide a general frame of reference by which accounting practice can be evaluated and (2) guide the development of new practices and procedures."[7] He recog-

2. William Andrew Paton, *Accounting Theory* (New York: Ronald Press, 1922), p. iii.

3. Paton, p. 472.

4. A. C. Littleton, *Essays in Accountancy* (Urbana-Champaign, Ill.: University of Illinois Press, 1961), p. 376. This passage was written in 1939.

5. Littleton, 1948 ed., p. 310.

6. Littleton, 1949 ed., p. 387.

7. Eldon S. Hendriksen, *Accounting Theory* (Homewood, Ill.: Richard D. Irwin, 1965), p. 1.

nizes that "accounting theory may also be used to explain existing practices to obtain a better understanding of them"[8] but subordinates this objective to that of providing "the general frame of reference for the evaluation and development of sound accounting practices."[9] Grounds for the choice of the one instead of the other do not seem to be explicitly given.

For Newman and Melman, "the entire framework of accounting theory and its concepts and principles can be viewed as constituting, in effect, the reporting principles and standards designed to achieve fairness in financial reporting."[10] Thus, for them, accounting theory is something *designed* and is, further, restricted to certain requirements of financial *reporting*. Since these authors set out to provide assistance for candidates for the CPA examinations, their attitude is presumably a reflection or at least a not uncommon interpretation of that of the professional body which conducts those examinations.

Leonard Spacek draws a distinction between the terms "practical" and "theoretical," "practical being usable or valuable in practice or action; while theory is contemplation or speculation."[11] He also averred that, "when theory and professional requirements to state facts are in conflict, the theory is wrong."[12] Thus, it would seem that theory has a normative or ethical character, if it can be right or wrong rather than true or false.

ARS (Accounting Research Study) no. 1, although not explicitly defining accounting theory, has an implicit interpretation of it as a set of statements called postulates "because . . . usage of the term lends itself readily to a systematic classification of the propositions of accounting theory and practice."[13] And in his comments on this study Mr. Spacek states that "the essential prerequisite to the establishment of a sound framework of accounting theory must be a clear determination of the purposes and objectives of accounting, which would

8. Hendriksen, p. 1.

9. Hendriksen, p. 1.

10. Benjamin Newman and Martin Melman, *Accounting Theory: A CPA Review* (New York: John Wiley and Sons, 1967), p. v.

11. Leonard Spacek, *A Search for Fairness in Financial Reporting to the Public* (Chicago: Arthur Andersen & Co., 1969), p. 171. This is strongly reminiscent of the definition in Samuel Johnson's Dictionary of 1785: *Theory*. Speculation, not practice; scheme; plan or system yet subsisting only in the mind.

12. Spacek, p. 182.

13. Maurice Moonitz, *The Basic Postulates of Accounting*, Accounting Research Study (ARS) 1 (New York: American Institute of CPA's [AICPA], 1961), p. 2.

go far beyond the 'definition of accounting' in Chapter 3. . . ." [14]

Mr. Spacek's views are further expressed in his comments on that study: "After the purposes and objectives of accounting are properly defined [and recognized as prerequisites to theory], the next step is the establishment of a basic foundation to accomplish these purposes and objectives. . . . Then, sound accounting principles consistent with that foundation should be determined."[15] The inference is that accounting theory is the basic foundation which is established to accomplish the purposes and objectives of accounting. And, in his comments on ARS 3, he states again: "The principal purpose of the two research studies . . . is to establish a sound foundation for and a general framework of accounting theory so that financial accounting and the resulting financial reporting will meet the current needs of all segments of our society."[16]

Another suggestion was made by Carman G. Blough, who, in commenting on ARS 3, stated: "Accounting principles are not theoretical hypotheses untried in practice or tried and discarded as impractical."[17]

The AAA Statement of Basic Accounting Theory (ASOBAT) states: "We define 'theory' as a cohesive set of hypothetical, conceptual and pragmatic principles forming a general frame of reference for a field of study,"[18] and "the committee has conceived of theory as a coherent set of concepts explaining and guiding the accountant's action in identifying, measuring and communicating economic information."[19] R. F. Salmonson puts these together and gets: "Accounting theory consists of a cohesive set of conceptual, hypothetical, and pragmatic propositions 'explaining and guiding the accountant's action in identifying, measuring, and communicating economic information.' "[20]

These last definitions suggest a few observations:

1. The whole set of "principles" (AAA), "concepts" (AAA), or "propositions" (Salmonson) comprises accounting theory. This does not appear to leave room for a theory of this or that, unless one equates a theory with a principle or a concept or a proposition. In other words, "accounting theory" in this use of the term is, of necessity, general.

14. Moonitz, p. 57.
15. Moonitz, p. 57.
16. Robert T. Sprouse and Maurice Moonitz, *A Tentative Set of Broad Accounting Principles for Business Enterprises*, ARS 3 (New York: AICPA, 1962), p. 77.
17. Sprouse and Moonitz, p. 60.
18. ASOBAT (Evanston, Ill.: AAA, 1966), p. 1.
19. ASOBAT, p. 2.
20. R. F. Salmonson, *Basic Financial Accounting Theory* (Bellmont, Calif.: Wadsworth Publishing Co., 1969), p. 1.

2. The principles, etc., have to be "cohesive" or "coherent," but it is not explained what is meant by these terms. Salmonson goes on to say that "the term 'proposition' is defined as any declarative statement, true or false. It is used to include in the body of theory ideas not universally acceptable, but advanced for explanation or for guidance of practice."[21] In the absence of further guidance from Salmonson, this seems to imply that some false statements and some true statements may be brought into a relation of cohesiveness with each other to give us the "body of theory." It is somewhat difficult to see the relevance of universal acceptability in this connection. What is meant by a declarative statement being either universally acceptable or not universally acceptable? Human nature being what it is, surely the great probability is that those who agree with it will accept it, while those who do not agree with it will not accept it. Where does that get us?

3. The principles, etc., are stated to be "hypothetical, conceptual and pragmatic." Does this mean that each principle, etc., is hypothetical, conceptual, and pragmatic at the same time? Or is it meant that some principles are hypothetical, some conceptual, and some pragmatic? And what meaning is attached to each of these adjectives?

4. The AAA committee, first, has the principles forming a general frame of reference for a field of study; later its concepts explain and guide the accountant's action. There seems to be some inconsistency here. Accountants' actions may be a field for study, and I believe they are, but the concepts which guide accountants in their actions may not be the same as the principles which constitute a frame for a field of study. If the committee had said in the first place that it was looking at a frame of reference for the actions of accountants, such a statement would at least have been consistent.

This is by no means an exhaustive listing of expressed views; the selection has been made simply to draw attention to the fact that there are conflicting views among writers on accounting as to what accounting theory is all about. Of course, each one of us no doubt knows what he means by accounting theory, but, viewed collectively, we do seem to have difficulty in making our meaning pellucid.

Theory Sense

Because it appeared that some confusion existed even then among writers on accounting theory, I drew a broad distinction some years ago between what I called "accounting doctrine" and "accounting

21. Salmonson, p. 1.

theory."[22] Briefly, the basis of that distinction was that in accounting theory we are concerned with *discovering* propositions of a generalizing nature which express facets of truth about the phenomena of accounting; whereas, in accounting doctrine we are interested in *propounding* or laying down standards which are to govern the activities of accountants in their work. Under this distinction, accounting theory deals with concepts, accounting doctrine with precepts; theory with examination of what is, doctrine with what should be.

I am still of the opinion that the distinction is valid and of sufficient significance to warrant the use of different expressions, but as I do not desire to quibble about the use of words, let us for present purposes call them both theory, but let us distinguish between Theory Sense 1 and Theory Sense 2. Theory Sense 1 is the desirable frame of reference now so often being referred to as the desideratum for governing the conduct and performance of accountants, especially in the preparation of reports of companies and corporations for public consumption. This is, to a large degree (but not wholly), equivalent to what I previously designated accounting doctrine. Theory Sense 2 carries the meaning of generalizations derived from observed phenomena of accounting. This is the sense in which accounting theory was used in the work referred to.

It is clear that Theory Sense 1 is the area that practitioners are most interested in. They are seeking guidance in the performance of their functions in a complex environment which has changed and is changing rapidly. The accelerated rate of change in the world in which the accountant operates has created problems which have arisen virtually unforeseen but which, nevertheless, often demand urgent solution. Some of these problems have been relatively short-lived, some have been solved, but many remain recalcitrant and almost impervious to the best endeavors of many accounting thinkers.

Hence, most of the attention of the relevant committees of the professional bodies of accountants, of leaders of the profession, and of many academic writers has been turned in this direction. These people have been seeking a set of propositions which will serve as a code by which accountants can fashion their performance and justify their professional stance. They have, so to speak, been trying to construct a set of instructions to accompany a do-it-yourself accounting kit. The story of this endeavor up to a fairly recent date has been told by

22. L. Goldberg, *An Inquiry into the Nature of Accounting* (Evanston, Ill.: AAA, 1965), pp. 34–35 and chaps. 3 and 4.

Reed K. Storey.[23] It is desirable, I think, to consider just a few basic aspects of this development.

It is surely important to be quite clear in our own minds as to what we are doing or trying to do. If we wish to derive standards of performance, we are in a normative field—an area of norms—and the basic question that we are asking is: What is good accounting? Or better, perhaps, what is the best accounting?

This is the area of ideals, the area of mores, the area of law—justice, equity, fairness. But it is also the area of personal disagreement, of preferences and prejudices, of differing interpretations, even of defiance and rebellion. It is the area of balancing the many against the few, benefit against detriment, advantage against disadvantage. Here belong the discussions of how general and how accepted generally accepted principles should be, and of what, in some countries of the British Commonwealth, is meant by "true and fair" in an auditor's opinion.

Limitations of time and space do not permit a full examination of the problems arising from these considerations, but there are two points of significance which should be commented upon.

First, if we wish to set up standards of performance, we must recognize that we *are* in a normative field, and considerations of ethics (as a field of study, not in the sense of professional behavior) are pertinent and warrant attention. And on this point I cannot express what I think is the appropriate attitude more aptly than in the words of a writer in a very different discipline:

> there have . . . been theories which have attempted to base ethics on natural science, and in particular on biology and psychology. But such theories appear to have been guilty, on occasions, of illogicality in that they appear to have assumed that ethical propositions can be deduced as a conclusion solely from non-ethical premises. . . .
>
> We cannot infer that we ought to do "x" from, for example, the statements "most people do x," or "most people desire to do x," or "most people are commanded to do x"; there must also be an acceptable ethical premise such as "we ought to do what other people do" or ". . . what other people desire to do" or ". . . what other people are commanded to do." Furthermore, this argument that we cannot draw an ethical conclusion from entirely non-ethical premises applies not only to psychology or biology; a system of moral precepts can not only have no complete de-

23. Reed K. Storey, *The Search for Accounting Principles* (New York: AICPA, 1964).

> pendence on science: it can have no complete dependence, for instance, on theology or history. Premises arrived at from such studies may, of course, lead to ethical conclusions, but only if one premise is itself ethical. Furthermore, such ethical premises must, of course, command the support of those concerned, and it has been at this point that many ethical theories have failed to carry conviction.[24]

Does this help to explain why there has been such great difficulty in arriving at the body of principles or postulates or standards—call them what you will—which should govern the performance of accountants? Have we led ourselves up a garden path in seeking norms from positive observations without recognizing the need for an intervening normative premise which can command support?

It may be that Mr. Spacek is right in saying that there is only one basic postulate for the guidance of accountants; but, if he is, has he chosen the right one? Let us consider for a few moments the proposed postulate of fairness. The implication seems to be that the accountant (Query: Is this meant to be the CPA only, or does it include others as well?) is in a position to determine what is fair for all parties concerned. This, in turn, implies that the accountant knows who all the parties are and what their requirements are in respect to accounting information. It should be noted also that this proposition seems to be related particularly to published information, although it might be suggested that internal data are also meant to be covered.

Now, if to be fair means to be impartial, that is, not to favor any person or group of persons vis-à-vis others, then this presumes that there is available neutral information uncolored by the influence of the interests of anybody. It is possible that accounting data of this kind do exist, especially, perhaps, in relation to events that have taken place in the past. But there is also, of necessity, a sizable quantum of accounting data that is not and cannot be free from the attitudes of particular people concerned in the quantification of prospective or even of some past events; this applies in any uncompleted venture at any given point of time.[25] However earnestly the accountant may wish to interpret these incomplete ventures impartially, or better perhaps, neutrally, he

24. Crawford Knox, *The Idiom of Contemporary Thought* (New York: Chapman and Hall, 1956), p. 150.

25. The term "venture" is here used in the same sense as in chap. 8 of my *An Inquiry into the Nature of Accounting*, viz., a series of events linked by a common measure and a social or economic objective into a meaningful relationship.

must adopt *somebody's* point of view about them. And this brings us straight up against the problems that accountants have been talking and writing about for years without having arrived at any complete solution—problems of valuation of assets, going-concern or break-up bases, depreciation and amortization, conservatism and consistency, price-level change, etc. It seems difficult to see how a criterion of fairness, in the sense of impartiality, would in fact make any difference to the tasks which the accountant has to face at present.

However, to be fair might have a somewhat different meaning, namely, to be equitable. At first sight, this might seem to be the same as being impartial, but in many cases equity requires some kind of compensation for a person or group of persons who may be at a disadvantage vis-à-vis others. That is to say, some kind of equalizing process is envisaged. Now, neutral information is not ipso facto of equal use or benefit to different people. If the accountant is to apply this notion of fairness as a criterion, his task will be even more onerous than under the other interpretation. Not only would he need to know who all the parties are and their requirements, he would also need to know whether any of them suffers any disabilities relative to others in interpreting information, what these are, and how to compensate for them, so that the *relative* disabilities would disappear. This would involve a knowledge of means of avoiding the perpetuation of the relation of such disabilities, for it is hard to see how information made publicly available would not benefit those with present advantages at least as much as those with present disadvantages, with the result that the latter would still be under a *relative* disability. Even if *all* available information were made known to *all* parties, the relative disability of inadequacy in interpretation would remain. The concept of equitableness imposes a judicial function upon the accountant which he is not adequately trained to carry out, especially when it comes down to specific cases, which it must do if it is to be of any practical significance. So long as social and / or economic and / or political activity is undertaken in any but the smallest and simplest communities, there must surely always be some people who know more about the activities of a particular unit than others, who may be affected by those activities. Equality of knowledge and even equality of opportunity for knowledge are mythical, even if only because of inevitable time lags between action and reporting upon action.

Of course, the term "fairness" may mean something different altogether; if it does, I am sure we should all be happy to consider it.

Perhaps the committee of the AICPA was right in stating that postulates were few in number[26] (although I find it hard to understand how they could know this unless they knew what they were); but perhaps, too, they were wrong in insisting that these postulates lay in the environment of accounting, for a person's norms of conduct and performance are the result of a self-development. He may develop them through the experience of his interactions with the circumstances in which he finds himself from time to time, but the important word here is "interaction"; that is, his development comes from a process of adaptation to his environment, but it is *he* who adapts. It may sound old-fashioned to talk about heredity and environment, but we all do still owe something of what we are to our parents and forebears. And I suggest that there is a sense in which a profession is in an analogous position; it has to find its norms within itself, that is, the actions of its members. The members of a profession should, indeed, study the environment in which the profession exists and they operate, but their norms cannot be wholly derived from that environment: the traditions of the profession should also play a part.

The second point is this: the standards of performance adopted, if they are to be effective, must be based upon somebody's authority and need to be supported by some sort of sanction. The acceptance of a code involves some sacrifice of freedom of action, and the question that arises is: are the members of the accountancy profession willing to yield their freedom of action to some other body, be it even a committee of their own choosing? Experience with one or two of the APB's opinions provides some evidence of doubt about the willingness to do this to the extent necessary.

Even a statute passed by a constitutionally authorized body will not be effective if a sufficiently strong body of opposition is marshalled against its operation. The floor of history is strewn with examples of authoritative pronouncements of various kinds which, because of sufficiently strong opposition to them, have had to be withdrawn, been allowed to become inoperative, or else have produced conditions of rebellion.

Numerous references have been made to the urgency for the profession to formulate its set of generally accepted principles for fear that some governmental agency would take the task into its own hands and do the job for the profession. This appears to be regarded with a considerable degree of horror. I wonder whether this fear is completely

26. See Moonitz, p. 1.

justified. Provided that responsible representations of the profession are seriously considered, I cannot see that the formulation of a code of performance by a governmental agency would *necessarily* be a bad code. It might well have the advantage of having been impartially constructed. And, if it were not a bad code, it would at least have the virtue of force of law and a system of enforceable sanctions to make it operative. But, of course, whoever formulates the code, the question is whether we trust our code-makers.

Theory Sense 2-A

Accounting (and, in earlier texts and articles, bookkeeping) has often been defined as or asserted to be a science. In most of such statements insufficient attention has been paid to the characteristics of either accounting or science to convince that the label fits properly.

More recently, argument has been put forward to justify the view that accounting makes use of scientific method. At times one gets an impression that it is not so much those who carry out the accounting processes who say this, but rather, those writers about accounting (including myself) who convince themselves of their own scientific integrity.

I do not wish to engage in the rather sterile "art or science" debate, but I think it is worth repeating that, even if accountants are not themselves scientific in their work, this does not preclude a scientific study of what they do. In the same way, the activities of primitive tribesmen or of subnormal people may not be scientific in the way in which we normally use that word, but this does not preclude a scientific study of their activities.

Very little is known—or at least has been recorded for us—about the way accountants do, in fact, go about their day-to-day work, so that we cannot judge whether they do attack their problems in a scientific way. Whatever evidence there is could well be collected and analyzed from this point of view.

I am aware, of course, that a great deal has been written and lectured on scientific method, and it is pretty good stuff. Much of it—perhaps most of it—has been written by philosophers and logicians, and I have quoted from it on occasions when it suited me. But, on this occasion, time does not permit a lengthy excursion into it.

However, we should remind ourselves that the essential characteristic of the practicing scientist (as distinct, perhaps, from the academic scientific methodist) is surely curiosity as to what is. He wants to find out something, preferably something which nobody knows yet. How something works in the way it does, why something exists in the way it does. The *why* is not a teleological why but an operational one; it is, in effect, an extended *how*. What is termed causal relationship, or necessary and sufficient conditions, and so on, is a statement of how x and y are related to each other.

The function of a theorist is to formulate statements which will enable people, including himself, to understand the relation between disparate phenomena. These phenomena—or facts—can only be perceived or observed; they have no theory content in themselves. But, when various facts are related to each other, the element of theory appears. That is, theory, as distinct from facts, arises when a relationship between two or more facts or series of facts is perceived or hypothesized. Such a relationship can be tested for its relative truth; that is, it can be confirmed or refuted. And we must not forget that this discernment, perception, or hypothesizing of a relationship is a human activity; hence, value judgment enters into it, and the influence of one's environment and habits of thought come into play. At the same time, we cannot talk about facts without expressing some relationships; the very naming of a fact is an expression of a lingual or semantic relationship between the word and the thing. It follows that value judgments and relationships and truth are inevitably and inextricably bound up with the process of communication.

The relevance of this is that it suggests that it is important to discover some general propositions about accounting as it is practiced, before finally writing prescriptions about the way it should be practiced. This is not to say, as some writers seem to argue, that what is being done now is satisfactory and should not be changed. It is to say that we should find out what is being done at present and why it is being done in the way it is. Apart from satisfying our scientific curiosity, the resulting understanding may provide a basis for formulating prescriptive statements as needed.

For example, it is not difficult to argue with a great deal of force, as many writers have done, that accountants (and businessmen) are wrong in their treatment—or rather nontreatment—of the problems arising out of so-called price-level changes. A significant question that still has not, so far as I am aware, been adequately answered is why they do what they do. Is it wholly and simply due to wrongheadedness and perverseness? Are they conscious and deliberate sinners flying in the face of divine authority—the divinity being the goddess of Reason? Or do they err through ignorance? Or through apathy? Or could it be that some people in business benefit through such changes? To get proper answers to these questions, we need empirical investigations into what is in fact happening, so that generalizations and diagnoses can be securely and convincingly based on a wealth rather than on a meager sample of evidence. It would be fruitful, I think, to ask directors and general managers questions such as these: are you aware of the fact that since the end of World War II the purchasing power of the dollar has declined steadily and considerably? If so, have you taken this decline into consideration in formulating your business policy? If so, what steps have you taken; if not, why haven't you taken any? Answers to questions like these would tell us something about what people do or don't do and why.

There are many, many questions that may be formulated that have not yet been asked as a basis for scientifically derived generalizations about the accounting process.

In other words, dispassionate fact-finding investigations are required, and they will be more convincing, in whatever direction they point, than polemics and assertions, however logically based these latter may be.

Briefly and in summary, the position I want to take is this: there is something to be found out about accounting, and it is embodied in what accountants do. Hence, we must observe what they do, try to measure it in some way, and try to develop hypotheses (i.e., statements of relationships) which can be tested by further observation. If, over a period, some generalizations can be firmly established by reference to observed and recorded data, we shall be on our way to developing some Sense 2-A theories.

Theory Sense 2-B

Theory Sense 2 thus means explanation of relationships between facts. But the ultimate success of a theory in this sense depends on its capacity to predict as well as to explain.

This aspect has not gone completely unnoticed in accounting literature. For instance, D. C. Phillips wrote recently: "Perhaps the most important feature of a scientific theory is its *predictive value*. With the aid of a theory it should be possible to make a prediction about some future observable event. Sir Karl Popper has explicated this predictive function of science in detail and he has argued that non-scientific theories (or pseudo-scientific theories) do not have predictive value."[27]

It must be remembered, however, that even what appear to be the most firmly based scientific theories are still tentative: they are founded on environmental assumptions which further investigation may show to have limitations in the scope of their application.

Nevertheless, the aim in any discipline which may be claimed to be scientific is to attain to propositions which are generalizations derived from the observation of phenomena and which can be used to predict phenomena. If the predicted occurrences take place in accordance with the inferences drawn from the propositions, this tends to confirm the generalization; if they do not, a re-examination of the generalization is clearly called for. For we must also recognize and remember that the facts of life are obstinate. They cannot be ignored indefinitely, nor can they be distorted to suit our convenience. But they can be explored. And I suggest that the facts of life with which the accounting observer is concerned are aspects of human behavior. A balance sheet, a funds statement, a statement of variances are expressions of the results of human activity. Certainly they are expressed in words and figures, but these are garments, so to speak, which clothe the activities of people and which, one might observe in passing, can be and often are styled and cut to make specific impressions.

If we wish to explore the possibilities of predictive theory in accounting, we shall have to be immodest enough to penetrate beneath the outer garment of reports and statements to the human behavior beneath them. I do not think this is impossible, although we have scarcely begun to do so as yet. When we do, who knows what wonders we may uncover.

At the same time, we must remember that many of the most fruitful discoveries in modern science have come from investigation into the nonconformity of observed phenomena to the predictions of their behavior.

Rationality and Priority

This leads to the consideration of two further points. The first is that in the literature of accounting—and of some other disciplines—much seems to have been made of rational behavior. Some expression about rationality almost always appears among our postulates. The meaning of this seems to have been largely taken for granted, and so

27. D. C. Phillips, "Systems Theory—A Discredited Philosophy," *Abacus* 5, no. 1 (Sept. 1969): 14.

also has the self-evidence of its existence and, indeed, of its universality.

On the first aspect—its meaning—I suggest that anybody who postulates rationality should make it clear in what sense he makes use of it, for it may mean different things to different people. For example, is a rational action one for which results conform to expectations held when the action was taken; or one that has been reasoned out; or one that has had a successful or pleasing outcome, whether expected or not; or one that is what a normal person would do in accordance with the mores of his society; or one that we think we ourselves would have taken in the same circumstances; or, simply, one that can be explained (whatever that may mean) to somebody's (perhaps our own) satisfaction?[28]

The philosophy underlying rationality seems to be that a rational person is someone like you and me, and, while there may conceivably be some doubt about you, there surely cannot be about me. But a great deal of human behavior, including economic behavior, is not based on what I would call a rational attitude. Consider some of the priorities of our social life. By what standard of rationality does a football coach earn much more than a university professor? Or a movie star than the secretary of the United Nations? Or a pop group more than the group of astronauts who reached the moon? And how much of our national advertising and marketing bill is directed towards promoting impulsive, rather than reasoned, buying? If you wish to accept these conditions of society as being based on rationality, you are welcome to do so, but please do not ask me to accept them without making it clear what kind of rationality embraces them.

On the second aspect—that of its universality—I cannot do better than quote a passage from R. G. Collingwood: "the idea that every agent is wholly and directly responsible for everything that he does is a naive idea which takes no account of certain important regions in moral experience. On the one hand, there is no getting away from the fact that men's characters are formed by their actions and experiences: the man himself undergoes change as his activities develop. On the other hand, there is the fact that to a very great extent people do not know what they are doing until they have done it, if then. The extent to which people act with a clear idea of their ends, knowing what effects they are aiming at, is easily exaggerated. Most human action is

28. For some questions that arise under each of these interpretations, see Louis Goldberg, "How Rational is Rational?" *New York Certified Public Accountant* (July 1964), p. 514.

tentative, experimental, directed not by a knowledge of what it will lead to but rather by a desire to know what will come of it."[29]

It might be observed that, based on this criterion, much of scientific development has not been rational, in that so many scientific discoveries have been accidental, by-products of activities directed to some end other than that resulting. Further, in the application of scientific method, the end envisaged as a result of deductive reasoning has to be tested by experiments or observations—often many of them—in which a process of trial and error, which is not very rational, is necessary.

The second point concerns the place of a priori reasoning. We all use a priori reasoning at times, that is, we deduce from the general to particulars, but if we are wise, we do not act on the conclusions so reached without checking them against the actual world. Hence, while the purely deductive reasoning process has a place in accounting theory, its limitations should be clearly recognized.

Now it seems to me that this sort of reasoning has had a very good run in the accounting literature in recent years. It is, of course, the basis of model building, and there can be nothing against this—we all do it at some time or other. Models are often such beautiful entities. But when it comes to formulating a set of axioms or postulates from which we deduce particular propositions which are intended to govern the actions of people, we must, I suggest, be very careful indeed about them. A few questions suggest themselves in relation to any basic postulate, axiom, or whatever other name it may go under.

1. Is it self-evident? If so, it amounts simply to an "I believe" assertion—a subjective evaluation supported by the background and experience of the person making the assertion and really acceptable only either to the credulous or to those with a similar background and experience; in other words, to those who are willing to accept it. We must be aware that what is self-evident to me may not be self-evident to somebody else now, or to me in a year's time. If we are to be scientific in our approach, we must remember that in the search for Truth there is no self-evident truth. The history of human thought is full of overthrown self-evident truths.

2. Is it something which is proved by practice? If so, then the evidence for it must be presented, complete and convincing, before acceptance should be expected.

3. Is it a conclusion arrived at in another area of study? If so, the

29. R. G. Collingwood, *The Idea of History* (Oxford: Clarendon Press, 1946), pp. 41–42.

basis for it in that other area needs to be examined rigorously and the previous questions asked in the context of that other area. If it is a conclusion arrived at in a science, we must bear in mind that scientists are very much aware that all their laws and theories are tentative.

4. Is it a definition? If so, it cannot produce more than it contains within itself by implication. A definition is usually a description rather than a premise.

If we seek to apply the rules of logic to a series of postulates, we must also bear in mind that a logical system is, of necessity, a closed system. As already argued, *ought* propositions cannot be derived *logically* from *is* propositions without the interposition of some other *ought* proposition. One of the virtues of using mathematics or symbolic logic is to discover the limitations of our postulates and our logic as well as their potentialities. As D. C. Phillips cogently put it: "the conclusion of a valid deduction cannot contain an expression that does not appear in the premises; this indeed is the core of the issue, because scientific explanations can be put in the form of deductions. It follows from this logical point that the possession of an emergent property cannot be deduced from premises that do *not* contain reference to this property; it is logically impossible, for example, to deduce the production of a colourless, odourless and tasteless liquid (i.e., water) from premises that refer only to the properties of the gaseous substances hydrogen and oxygen."[30]

Many writers, at least since Francis Bacon, have warned against the dangers of over-reliance on a priori reasoning. One of the most graphic commentaries was made by John Tyndall in 1874, and, although it is of ancient vintage and refers to an even more ancient scientist-philosopher, it seems worth citing in part, if only for the felicity of its language:

"As a physicist, Aristotle displayed what we should consider some of the worst attributes of a modern physical investigator—indistinctness of ideas, confusion of mind, and a confident use of language, which led to the delusive notion that he had really mastered his subject, while he had as yet failed to grasp even the elements of it. He put words in the place of things, subject in the place of object. He preached Induction without practising it, inverting the true order of inquiry by passing from the general to the particular, instead of from the particular to the general. He made of the universe a closed sphere, in the centre of which he fixed the earth, proving from general prin-

30. Phillips, p. 14.

ciples, to his own satisfaction and to that of the world for near 2,000 years, that no other universe was possible. . . . He affirmed that a vacuum could not exist, and proved that if it did exist motion in it would be impossible. He determined *a priori* how many species of animals must exist, and showed on general principles why animals must have such and such parts. . . . Aristotle's errors of detail . . . were grave and numerous. He affirmed that only in man we had the beating of the heart, that the left side of the body was colder than the right, that men have more teeth than women, and that there is an empty space at the base of every man's head."[31]

Conclusion

Accounting, in the sense of the sort of work accountants do, may, if you wish, be regarded as an art. If it is so regarded, it is an art of selection, analysis, interpretation, design, and presentation. In this respect, it is proper to formulate standards of performance.

At the same time, the processes involved in this so-called art can be examined dispassionately and scientifically, and, it is to be hoped, some valid generalizations, that is, statements of tendency, may be formulated.

Perhaps the confusion (as I see it) arises from the fact that the subject matter in both cases is the same, namely, human behavior. But in the one case—the search for standards of performance—the search is for an ethic. In the other—the quest for relationships between phenomena—the search is for (tentative) truth. Both are needed, but they are different things and should not be mixed up in our minds.

I am very conscious of many limitations in this paper. In particular, it oversimplifies the position and deals very broadly with problems which need to be examined in much greater detail than has been possible in the present context. This is a need whose complete satisfaction will require the efforts of many people for a considerable period. Nevertheless, I have tried to state the essence of the problem of accounting theory as I see it and to disentangle some of the knots in thinking that we seem to have made for ourselves.

At the same time, I recognize that some valuable and exciting empirical research work has recently been carried out and is currently being carried out, particularly by some of the younger people in our ranks. This is an encouraging development, and we should try to foster the

31. John Tyndall, *Address Delivered Before the British Association Assembled at Belfast, 1874* (London: Longmans Green & Co.), p. 14.

work of such investigators, for, in my view, it is on them that the hope for the future of our profession rests.

One point I should like to emphasize, in conclusion, is that, so far as I am concerned, the examination of what is does not imply that what is, is right. It simply means that what is, is there—to be examined and explored and explained and understood. And all this by whatever means of enquiry are appropriate and productive.

Finally, I end as I began, with a short sentence from William James: "Theories thus become instruments, not answers to enigmas, in which we can rest."[32]

32. James, p. 53.

Comments on "Varieties of Accounting Theory"

Stephen A. Zeff

SAMUELSON WRITES, "Methodological discussion, like calisthenics and spinach, is good for us."

It was not until the 1950s (with a few earlier exceptions) that accounting writers evinced an interest in the content and structure of theory. Shortly after the transoceanic exchange of pointed criticisms between Chambers and Littleton, a special committee of the AICPA thrust the word "postulates" into the center of accounting controversy. The emphasis of the institute's new research program on deductive reasoning[1] seemed to be precipitated by mounting frustration with the "pragmatic-prescriptive" approach of the Committee on Accounting Procedure. Under the new plan, postulates were the lock and research was the key that would open the way toward resolving the alleged internal inconsistencies and blurred focus of accounting practice.

With few exceptions, accounting researchers in the 1960s placed the

1. I accept Moonitz' statement that both deductive and inductive processes will be found "in any inquiry other than the most abstruse speculations of metaphysics." Maurice Moonitz, "Why Do We Need 'Postulates' and 'Principles'?" *The Journal of Accountancy* (Dec. 1963), p. 45. When the terms "deductive" and "inductive" are used in this paper, it should be understood that the word "predominantly" stands in a shadow as a modifier.

deductive approach in a normative frame. Storey probably spoke for many of his brethren when he wrote: "A . . . proposition that should be laid to rest is that the purpose of accounting principles is to justify accounting practice. . . . A rationalizing effort is not properly termed 'research' for its intent is to defend existing conditions, whether good or bad, and is the antithesis of a search for the truth."[2]

Yet the new research movement brought its own brand of frustration. A number of deductive studies have appeared in the last ten years. They describe themselves as problem-oriented, postulational, axiomatic, or conceptual. Differences in terminology (which has never been a strong point in accounting practice or research), methodology, and rigor have made comparison and evaluation difficult. After assessing a recent deductive study, Caplan was moved to remark: "Recent experience . . . suggests that global theoretical formulations which are broad enough to receive widespread support are *too* broad to serve as workable guides to action. On the other hand, by the time that these formulations have been narrowed to the point where they might provide such guides, so many value judgments and unsupported assertions have been introduced that it is no longer possible to obtain agreement on the validity of the theory. Thus, in our opinion, if research in basic accounting theory is to be truly productive, it is necessary to concentrate efforts elsewhere."[3]

As we emerge from our first cycle of attempts at normative-deductive research, the voice of Louis Goldberg, a persistent spokesman for the apparently small school of empiricists among us, is beginning to attract attention.

I have traced Goldberg's Baconian leanings to his 1939 book *A Philosophy of Accounting* (which was revised in 1957 under the title *An*

2. Reed K. Storey, *The Search for Accounting Principles* (New York: AICPA, 1963), pp. 64–65. If Storey purports to imply that research may not play the role of observing the behavior of accountants and the behavior of those whose actions are reflected in accounting measurements, all with a view toward producing generalizations about the present state of the accounting function, I would charge that he defines research much too narrowly. It would appear, however, that Storey is complaining about the addition of value judgments to such generalizations in order to rationalize the perpetuation of observed accounting practices. Naturally, these value judgments are the product of an implicit normative-deductive analysis.

3. Edwin H. Caplan, "Relevance—A 'Will-o'-the-Wisp,'" *Abacus* (Sept. 1969), p. 53. Sterling, however, after reviewing the same study, concluded, "I agree with the new methodology and world-view." Robert R. Sterling, "A Statement of Basic Accounting Theory: A Review Article," *Journal of Accounting Research* (Spring 1967), p. 111.

Outline of Accounting). In a 1963 article Goldberg the skeptic is not impressed with the work being done in accounting theory.[4] In 1965 the AAA published his monograph *An Inquiry into the Nature of Accounting*, the first part of which is a statement of his methodological posture. It is there that he distinguishes between theory and doctrine, the latter being prescription by an authority "whose pronouncements are either respected or feared."[5] "Some writers," Goldberg writes, a bit pointedly, "think that deduction alone is the most powerful instrument in the advancement of knowledge."[6] Goldberg accepts deductively derived propositions that find referents in the world of experience, or fact. Failing such a test, a deductive proposition "must, for all purposes of *practical and practicable* application, remain barren, no matter how convincing the process of logical expression may be."[7]

In his paper presented at this conference Goldberg begins by demonstrating that the term "theory" means different things to different researchers. Even Hatfield, an eclectic who excelled at detecting illogic and incongruity in the accounting literature, would have liked Goldberg's low-profile conclusion: "viewed collectively, we do seem to have a little difficulty in making our meaning [of theory] pellucid." Goldberg's survey deftly reveals the conscious and unconscious methodological division among accounting researchers. Few writers other than Chambers, Deinzer, Devine, Littleton,[8] and Goldberg have probed the apparently bottomless depths of methodology as applied to accounting–if, indeed, accounting differs in this respect from other fields of study.

In the central part of his paper Goldberg classifies so-called theory into two senses. Theory Sense 1, which he still prefers to call doctrine, embraces the normative-deductive approach, including the ethical approach, which is separately classified by Moonitz, Hendriksen, and

4. Louis Goldberg, "The Present State of Accounting Theory," *The Accounting Review* (July 1963), pp. 457–69.

5. Louis Goldberg, *An Inquiry into the Nature of Accounting* (Iowa City: AAA, 1965), p. 35.

6. *An Inquiry into the Nature of Accounting*, p. 74.

7. *An Inquiry into the Nature of Accounting*, p. 76.

8. See the recent collection of Chambers' papers: R. J. Chambers, *Accounting, Finance and Management* (Chicago: Arthur Andersen & Co., 1969), esp. pp. 347–471; Harvey T. Deinzer, *Development of Accounting Thought* (New York: Holt, Rinehart and Winston, 1965); Carl Thomas Devine, "Research Methodology and Accounting Theory Formation," *The Accounting Review* (July 1960), pp. 387–99; and A. C. Littleton, *Structure of Accounting Theory* (Urbana, Ill.: AAA, 1953). See also the syntheses by Hendriksen and Salmonson, cited in footnote 9, *infra*.

Salmonson.[9] Theory Sense 2 refers to inductive or generalizing theory, and, if I may interpolate from his *Nature of Accounting Theory*, it would seem to admit deductive reasoning, in the positivist rather than normativist sense, the conclusion of which could be verified by empirical test. The A and B subdivisions of Theory Sense 2 distinguish between the explanative and predictive capacities of positive theory. The latter is an innovation in Goldberg's writing.

The issue is whether new knowledge in accounting should be supplied by normative or positive investigation: "what ought to be" versus "what is." This does not parallel the centuries-old debate among philosophers of science on rationalism versus empiricism. Nor will one find a direct parallel with the methodological dispute in economics, involving, among others, Friedman, Machlup, and Samuelson.[10] Their differences lie entirely within positivist theory, though some benefit can be derived from their discussions on whether the adequacy of (positivist) theory may be judged by the realism of its assumptions or by the predictive quality of the derived propositions or hypotheses.

Goldberg's empiricism is not identical to Littleton's special interpretation of inductivism. To his observations of experience, Littleton adds value judgments about the content of good and bad practice.[11]

Nor can Goldberg's empiricism be seen in Grady's *Inventory*.[12] Grady found real-world support for his basic concepts, objectives, and principles by drawing on SEC Accounting Series Releases, official pronouncements of policy-making committees of the AICPA, and the eighth edition of a widely known auditing book. As far as I can discern, Grady did not observe what accountants actually do. His sources of information are the quintessence of Goldberg's authority figure for propagating doctrine. Grady's inductive-like synthesis consists of a

9. Maurice Moonitz, *The Basic Postulates of Accounting* (New York: AICPA, 1961), pp. 3–4; Eldon S. Hendriksen, *Accounting Theory* (Homewood, Ill.: Richard D. Irwin, 1965), pp. 8–10; and R. F. Salmonson, *Basic Financial Accounting Theory* (Belmont, Calif.: Wadsworth Publishing Co., 1969), pp. 10–12.

10. See Milton Friedman, *Essays in Positive Economics* (Chicago: University of Chicago Press, 1953), pp. 3–34; and the several papers found in *Papers and Proceedings of the Seventy-fifth Annual Meeting of the American Economic Association* (Dec. 27–29, 1962); *American Economic Review* (May 1963), pp. 204–36; and the comments in *The American Economic Review* (Dec. 1965), pp. 1151–72.

11. For corroborating assessments, see Deinzer, pp. 56–57 and 145–46; and Chambers, esp. p. 366; and R. J. Chambers, "Some Observations on 'Structure of Accounting Theory,'" *The Accounting Review* (Oct. 1956), pp. 584–92.

12. Paul Grady, *Inventory of Generally Accepted Principles for Business Enterprises* (New York: AICPA, 1965).

number of generalizations derived from various levels of doctrine. That the recommendations of his authoritative sources are generally followed in accounting practice is a hypothesis that may be put to empirical test. But it is not empiricism to look only at the dictates of authority.

Nor is the Goldberg brand of empiricism to be found in Sterling's recent analytical survey of the nature and meaning of the term "going concern."[13] His field work is confined to the nonempirical accounting literature. The study does not observe what accountants actually do.

On the surface it would seem that the 1938 monograph *A Statement of Accounting Principles*, by Sanders, Hatfield, and Moore, approximates the Goldberg vision of empiricism. The authors report that inquiries were made of competent persons by means of "personal interviews, supplemented by correspondence."[14] Yet they also looked at the literature and were strongly influenced, in some sections, by evolving corporate law. Moreover, the accounting principles were expressed as imperatives, suggesting the intervention of value judgments.

Gilman's *Accounting Concepts of Profit* cannot qualify as empiricism, for it also draws on a largely nonempirical literature.

This brief review does not denigrate the usefulness of any of the research studies mentioned. It serves only to point out that much of our inductive research has not involved the observation of the accountant at work. There are instances, especially in doctoral research, of questionnaire surveys made of practicing accountants.[15] Though observation need not be personal observation, the probitive potential of studies limited to questionnaire surveys is often severely limited.

With Devine, I readily admit that research of the empirical mold is difficult to carry out and necessarily entails a great deal of subjectivity in design and execution.[16]

In discussing Goldberg's Theory Sense 1, I think we must distinguish, at least at the level of conception, between two types of normative-deductive research found in the accounting literature. On the one hand, we have suffered argument by authority, argument by

13. Robert R. Sterling, "The Going Concern: An Examination," *The Accounting Review* (July 1968), pp. 481–502.

14. Thomas Henry Sanders, Henry Rand Hatfield, and Underhill Moore, *A Statement of Accounting Principles* (New York: American Institute of Accountants, 1938), p. xv.

15. A recent and noteworthy example is Abraham J. Briloff, *The Effectiveness of Accounting Communication* (New York: Frederick A. Praeger, 1967).

16. Devine, pp. 393–94.

tradition and usage ("it is good because it is done"), and, most important, argument by deduction with unstated assumptions. "The actual state of accounting," writes Chambers, "is not that it has no theories, but that it has an almost inexhaustible quantity of implicit, partial, and contradictory theories."[17] This implicitness makes it impossible to monitor the validity of argument. It is more religion than theology.

The second type of normative-deductive research is that which makes explicit the antecedent propositions, attempts to demonstrate their concordance with environmental reality, and adheres to acceptable rules of logical inference.[18] The logical outcome of this normative deduction would not necessarily correspond with the reality of extant accounting practice, yet the proposed accounting practices might be demonstrated to achieve the objectives implicit in the assumptions of the model.[19]

Here we encounter a fundamental difference between Goldberg and many normative deductivists. Goldberg's search for the truth in accounting would not be confined to what accountants do and what they say about what they do. Both Goldberg and the deductivists place emphasis on the impact of accounting on the behavior of persons who are not accountants. They may be investors, managers, creditors, or government officials, among others. While Goldberg's principal concern with the impact of accounting on the behavior of nonaccountants is in the predictive sphere—an important and worthy concern in itself—the normative deductivists are more directly concerned with the shape of accounting in the light of the needs it should satisfy. Accounting, being a service activity, must endeavor to discover and serve the needs of the community. In mediating the competing claims of different groups for his services, the accountant cannot escape making ethical judgments. Yet Goldberg believes that accountants are not able to make such decisions and, further, that ethical judgments are beyond the domain of science. Churchman, on the other hand, gives hope that science may yet cope with the ethical *oughts*. He writes:

17. Raymond J. Chambers, *Accounting, Evaluation, and Economic Behavior* (Englewood Cliffs, N.J.: Prentice-Hall, 1966), p. 371.

18. The most complete example of this type of study is the aforementioned *Accounting, Evaluation, and Economic Behavior.*

19. This type of proof is very difficult to attain in accounting. Writes Chambers: "since accounting is practised in a social matrix, the elements of which (habits, laws, regulations) cannot either be altered or held constant for the purpose of testing a new idea, the conclusions from any attempt to experiment with accounting ideas are likely to be vitiated by the numerous concurrent extraneous influences." Chambers, *Accounting, Finance and Management*, p. 381.

> ethical judgments are really judgments made for the sake of future generations. . . . The vague scientific interpretation of "X ought to do A on ethical grounds" is "A is what future man will want X to have done." Some of the vagueness of this translation has been removed by giving a tentative interpretation of "Y wants X to do A," where Y is a social group. If Y is the social group which includes future man, as the argument seems to demand, then the difficulties of explaining the idea of social approval become very great. . . .
>
> In a sense, the attempt to view morality through the eyes of science is more fantastic than factual, more visionary than precise. Science still knows so little about what present-day man wants that it is fantastic to talk about what future man will want, and to suggest the possibility of forecasting such wants by scientific method. Nevertheless, it is hard not to talk in this vein even though in so doing one drastically violates the ideals of rigor and clarity. It is difficult not to because science has a stake in morality, that is, in the future wants of humanity. Philosophers of science must ask themselves whether the problems of future men—admittedly relevant to current science—are forever beyond the understanding of current science.
>
> It therefore seems clear that we must consider the feasibility of a scientific discipline which predicts the future interests of men by means of a theory of the development of interests. Such a theory is much like discussions of the origin and ultimate fate of our universe—terribly important but not rigorously defensible at the present time.[20]

I believe that accountants *must* be interested in discovering the societal needs for their services. Present accounting practice, being no less need-oriented than some prospective and untried accounting practices, has supposedly evolved in response to demands and counterdemands, some expressed through formal law and its application, some communicated through less formal media. Through the prism of Goldberg's empiricism, and perhaps with the aid of a historical tracing of the point and counterpoint between accounting and its environment, we might discover the needs which present accounting practice strives to satisfy. Today, because of the dearth of historical and Goldberg-type empirical research in accounting, we can only speculate on the present condition.

20. C. West Churchman, *Prediction and Optimal Decision* (Englewood Cliffs, N.J.: Prentice-Hall, 1961), pp. 22 and 23–24.

Whatever the mix of societal needs that present-day accounting practice purports to satisfy, it should not be concluded without further study, first, that this group of needs is the best selection from the set of all possible needs and, second, that present accounting practice is adequate to satisfy the needs thus selected.

Though I have attempted to argue that normative deductivism deserves an important place in accounting research, I hasten to Goldberg's side as a fellow positivist. I fear that the pressures upon accounting researchers to invent better information systems to feed the insatiable appetite of sophisticated decision models have almost eclipsed the concern for accumulating knowledge, qua knowledge, about our field of study.

In our rush to convert accounting into an omnipotent information system to serve mankind's decision models, we should not ignore man's experience with accounting and the lessons that may be learned from such experience. The practice of accounting has a history and a present, and we as scholars know precious little about each. Historical investigations have been sparse, and some of these have been used as foils to prove the authors' preconceived notions. For accountants, we keep poor records; the records we have are seldom studied.

I therefore join Goldberg in the quest for what is, and I add for what has been.

But I cannot desist without submitting to a Machiavellian urge: Goldberg's empirical approach can conceivably play a strategic role in conditioning the practicing profession to the rigor of accounting research.

Goldberg says that " 'Theory Sense 1' is the area that practitioners are most interested in." Contrariwise, I would argue that the practitioners' growing frustration with the prescriptive literature, both authoritative and nonauthoritative, was what prompted the leaders of the profession to propose the AICPA's new research program twelve years ago.

Notwithstanding the use of the term "postulate" and the clear preference for the normative-deductive approach in the report of the institute's Special Committee on Research Program, I seriously doubt that the practicing profession at this time is intellectually or emotionally prepared to endeavor to understand and appreciate rigorously deductive studies of the normative type. At the present time there is a craving, I think, for general statements (they might be called principles by some) of what is. I would offer as evidence the popularity of the Grady *Inventory* in comparison with the reception accorded the normative Moonitz and Sprouse/Moonitz studies.[21]

A profession that has lived by authoritative prescription and religious dogmatism for many years cannot suddenly adapt to the enlightenment of normative scholarship—especially at a time when auditors' liability is one of the most unsettled areas in the law. In some circles, the word "theoretical" is the death blow to attempts to reform accounting. Theory is seen as a threat, and I suspect that the empiricism espoused by Goldberg, in addition to the obvious benefits its application would bring to the body of accounting knowledge, would at the present time command the greatest respect from practitioners. At the same time as it escapes the charges of promoting impractical and untried practices, it will, it is to be hoped, foster confidence among practitioners in the methodology of scientific investigation. Whether this degree of confidence will ever rise to the point where the profession would openly and dispassionately evaluate normative models is not presently known.

21. See the "Statement of the Accounting Principles Board (APB)," dated April 13, 1962, plus the comments of Barr, Blough, Grady, and Werntz in the Sprouse / Moonitz study. For the Grady study, see Anthony's book review, *The Accounting Review* (Jan. 1966), pp. 194–96; and Weldon Powell (who was the first chairman of the APB), "Inventory of Generally Accepted Accounting Principles," *The Journal of Accountancy* (Mar. 1965), pp. 29–35. See also Weldon Powell, "The Development of Accounting Principles," *The Journal of Accountancy* (Sept. 1964), pp. 37–43.

The Commercial Foundations of Accounting Theory

R. J. Chambers

THE LAST DECADE has seen the adequacy of existing methods of accounting, and their products, brought sharply into question. Around the world, commercial events, business failures, and the merger movement have obliged regulatory bodies to give more attention to the financial publicity provisions of the company codes than in any other decade. In the same decade there have been many symposia on accounting theory. Ten years ago we might have hoped that there would have emerged by now some clear and positive line of thought, some conclusions which would warrant the advancement with confidence of improvements in technique. There has been no such result.

Had it been a matter of only ten years, we could perhaps excuse ourselves. But the criticisms of Canning, Sweeney, and Macneal of some thirty to forty years ago have not been met, either in the general body of theory or in practice. I believe this failure to be explicable in terms of the modes of inquiry and exposition which have prevailed and seem to still prevail in accounting. For, first, there is a noticeable reluctance to assign quite definite and limited functions to accounting. Attempts to limit the field of discourse and the function of accounting proper are treated almost with scorn by teachers as well as practitioners. Yet, it was only when naturalists gave up mixing metaphysics with physics, and concentrated on a limited range of phenomena and ideas, that they laid the foundation of modern scientific knowledge. When one has mastered one's own speciality, it is profitable to consider what greater power, knowledge, or service it may in future put within one's grasp. But it is futile to adopt the role of visionary unless one knows how first to get rid of the follies of present doctrine and practice.

Second, almost everyone seems to think he is entitled to an opinion on the subject matter and the nature of accounting theory—an opinion, what is more, which others will respect. This belief may have been fostered by the prominence given to opinion and judgment in statements on practices. However, there can be no more mischievous idea than that the choice of the magnitudes recorded and reported and the choice of rules of processing are matters of opinion. There can be no greater source of disruption and confusion. For if these things are matters of opinion, there can be no solid core of principles, no ascertainable function, no systematic knowledge. It should be well known that it is profitless to debate matters of opinion. But to a considerable extent the literature consists of free-wheeling debate rather than the systematic, intensive, and consciously controlled analysis of present and proposed schemes of accounting.

Reluctance to assign precise and limited functions to accounting and an easy attitude toward the merit of mere opinion have doubtless contributed to the present methodological chaos. There has been relatively little accumulation of factual evidence, or recourse to available factual evidence, in the derivation of basic ideas. There has been much talk of the use of deduction,[1] but there is little evidence of its use. Some have attempted to align thinking about accounting with thinking about "economic matters" in the wider sense of the term. The phenomena under consideration have been described in such general terms that no clear accounting rules can be deduced.[2] Some have felt it impossible to proceed to clear conclusions, protesting ignorance of how people behave in commercial situations.[3] Some, while restricting at-

1. E.g., Carl Thomas Devine, "Research Methodology and Accounting Theory Formation," *The Accounting Review* (July 1960); Maurice Moonitz, *The Basic Postulates of Accounting* (New York, 1961), p. 6; Eldon S. Hendriksen, *Accounting Theory* (Homewood, Ill., 1965), chap. 1.

2. The use of such portmanteau terms as communication, measurement, resource, entity, information, environment, *without* any description or analysis of what is meant, is so common that it needs no documentation.

3. E.g., AAA, *A Statement of Basic Accounting Theory* (Evanston, Ill., 1966), p. 69. Perhaps the statement reflects the views of only some of its authors; see

tention to the actions of individuals and firms, have found it impossible to avoid mixing commercial, political, and psychic elements of choice and behavior.[4] And hardly anywhere is there presented evidence, from commercial and financial affairs, of the necessity of the information it is proposed that accounting should produce. In all, the linkage of theory with practical affairs, both at the initial postulational stage and at the final testing stage, is at best tenuous, and at worst missing altogether.

I have chosen to use the words "commercial foundations" in the title of this paper, first, because in my view accounting is concerned strictly with commercial experiences, events, and considerations; second, because to concentrate on specific particulars enables us to follow exactly the same course as others have followed in the pursuit of certain, or highly probable, generalized knowledge. I could as well have used the words "economic foundations" or "empirical foundations." I rejected them, because I wished to leave in no doubt my concern with specific particulars, the consideration of which, alone, can yield grounds for belief and tests of belief in one kind of accounting or another.

Events and Records

Much of the discussion of accounting deals in a general way with commercial affairs, buying, selling, borrowing, lending, and so on. But by far the greater part of it deals with the *records* of commercial affairs. Commercial affairs and the records of commercial affairs are not the same thing. A record is a construction, an artefact. The way it is constructed depends on how we see or understand the matters recorded and on how the matters recorded are subsequently to be seen or understood. A purchase, a sale, simply occurs. It can be recorded in many ways, from the long descriptive paragraphs of the early bookkeepers to the abbreviated symbols of mechanical devices. If it is an isolated event, it is sufficient to describe it as it occurred. But if it is part of an on-going mixed sequence of events, the consequences of which affect later choices and commercial dealing, it must be so em-

Norton M. Bedford, "The Nature of Future Accounting Theory," *The Accounting Review* (Jan. 1967); and George H. Sorter, "An 'Events' Approach to Basic Accounting Theory," *The Accounting Review* (Jan. 1969).

4. As witness, the rising occurrence in the literature of references to organizational and individual goals and social ends and values, in wider senses than the commercial or financial sense.

bedded in the record of those events that subsequently the effects of the mixture and the sequence can be seen and understood.

That a record is a construction is emphasized. If I keep a cash book, the balance it shows of cash on hand at any time is not necessarily the amount of cash I have. I and everyone else can make errors and lose money accidentally. The amount of money I have, not the amount in the cash book (unless the amounts are the same), determines what I can buy, and the usefulness to me of any reckoning I make before buying. If I keep a more complex record of cash movements and other movements in the things I buy, use, and sell for my own purposes, I am at liberty to do as I please—on the record. But, as in the case of the cash book, that record will only be indicative of what has happened and what I can now do if it is constructed with that object, and if in fact I have taken care to see that it records *all* the events which have affected my present capacity, and knowledge of which may affect my present judgment in respect of my commercial affairs.

I hope everyone would assent to the propriety of the two conditions mentioned. Whatever my likes and dislikes may be about the manner of keeping records, they cannot be allowed to affect the substance of the record if the product of the record is to help me in the two ways specified. If I choose to disregard any event or class of events which has had a bearing on my present capacity for buying, selling, borrowing, lending, paying debts, and so on, the statement of capacity which I deduce from the record will be inconsistent with my actual capacity. Similarly, if I choose to incorporate in the record any *expected* event or class of events which *may* in the future affect my capacity for commercial action, the deduced statement of capacity at any time will not be consistent with my actual capacity at that time. In both cases, my present judgments about the past and the possibilities of the present and the future will be mistaken if I base them on the statement deduced from the record.

I hope everyone would assent to these two propositions. I mention them because both the exclusion of things that have happened and the inclusion of things that are expected to happen seem to be countenanced by many extant and proposed practices. It is not denied that men may wish to classify past events the better to make judgments about the future. But classifying past events does not mean disregarding the effects of some of them. Nor is it denied that men may wish to speculate about future events, the better to choose which will serve them best. But speculation about the future does not warrant the introduction, into any statement of present capacity, of the substance of those speculations or of any one of them.

It seems highly probable that the confusion of past, present, and future in present and proposed practices has arisen because, in personal affairs, we very seldom have to think very closely about the distinction. We are familiar with our past experiences—at least we think we are. We are familiar with our present state; as individuals we have a rough idea at any time of the commercial worth of what we own. The thing that looms largest in our minds is thinking about what we might do next; how much will it cost us to have that vacation, furnish that room, run that additional car, and so on.

In business affairs, however, the things done are so numerous that only a small proportion of them comes under the notice of managers, and the experience of only that proportion is known to them. And none of them is known to investors and other outsiders. The effects of those and all other things must be brought together in some way which represents the whole experience of the firm. Similarly, the assets and obligations are generally so numerous that an account of them all must be prepared deliberately, if managers and investors are to be familiar with the present state of the firm. Certainly what the firm might do in the future is of consequence, as in the case of individuals thinking of their own affairs. But the discovery of what has occurred and of the resulting present position provides the major factual premises, of a financial kind, for speculation about the future. It cannot be brushed aside as readily as we might brush it aside in our personal affairs because of our own familiarity with those personal affairs. We hold this process of discovery to be the prime function of accounting. If it is not done as well as is possible, judgments about past and future lack that contact with the factual present which alone provides a trustworthy foundation for choice and action.

Commercially Necessary Information

There can be little doubt that the present states of business firms from time to time are of immediate concern to managers, at least in some obvious respects. Knowledge of cash flows, for example, is widely said to be of consequence. Anyone familiar with the care and attention given to cash positions, arrangements with bankers, short-term borrowing and lending, and such matters, by company treasurers and boards of directors, will know that in this respect what the literature says is matched by what is done in commercial practice.

Balances of receivables and payables are closely linked to cash balances. It would be futile to attempt to project cash movements from any point of time without firm knowledge of the cash balances and receivables and payables balances at that point of time. It would be equally futile to attempt to explain the past drift in net monetary balances without firm knowledge of those balances at the moment of the attempt.

For cash resources, firms are not limited to the amounts they can generate by way of revenues. They may pledge assets, singly or in total, as security for cash advances. The immediate security for lenders is the market selling price of the assets pledged. It is often said that the significant value of an asset to a firm is its calculated net present value in its present use. But no lender on the security of the firm's assets is concerned with the value of those assets to the firm in this sense. He is concerned with the value of those assets as generators of cash for himself in the event that he must enforce his claim against the borrower by sale of the charged asset. Furthermore, a borrower in this position will want to know the market prices of his assets in order to be free to make his own choice of arrangements to meet his creditors, so that he is not entirely at their mercy if he is unable to meet his obligations from ready cash.

For confirmation of this view, one may have recourse to bond indentures and similar instruments. Wherever a charge over particular assets or groups of assets is given as security for borrowings, there will be found some provision restricting other borrowing by reference to the amount of the assets of the borrower. Now the term "the amount of the assets" in such an indenture can have only one kind of meaning. The object of the provision is to cover the amount borrowed. This cover is given, not by the book values of assets, however determined, but by the market values of assets. It would be unwarranted to regard "the amount of the assets" as a term of art, having a meaning derived solely from accounting rules, whatever they might be. As we have said, a record is a construction. Unless what it yields is consistent with the real state of affairs, creditors' interests, in financial information for their protection, cannot be served. Nor indeed can the interests of borrowers be served.

There is ample evidence in the history of commerce of the correctness of the point we are making. A very simple and almost everyday instance is the buying of stock on margin. It must be widely known that if the market price of a stock bought on margin falls, the buyer must pay up, put up further security, or be sold out. On a more extensive level, there are many cases in which book values, which seemed to provide adequate cover for secured loans, have been found to be entirely misleading, to the very great cost of creditors.

It may be contended that lenders are accustomed to lend only a certain proportion of the amount of any pledged assets. But the safety margin can only be known to be safe if at any time the market value of pledged assets is known. Further, few firms have only one creditor. If a firm has only one creditor, and that creditor is sufficiently important to the firm to oblige it to disclose the market value of its assets, perhaps it would not matter (at least for the creditor's protection) that its balance sheet did not disclose the market values of its assets. But the typical situation is that a firm has many creditors, some secured, some unsecured. And all are entitled to know whether they may reasonably expect their claims to be met. Private disclosure of market values of assets to a few privileged creditors would not cover this case. Nor would it be possible for stockholders to judge whether or not a firm is approaching the limits of its borrowing power if they are in ignorance of the market prices of assets; yet, for any informed opinion on the prospects of changes in leverage and asset backing, this information is necessary.

Consider now the stockholders of a company. It would be generally agreed that the relative worths of two ventures determine which is to be preferred. Every classroom exercise and every real-life exercise in choosing between alternative investments has somewhere in it a present amount of cash or cash substitutes or cash equivalents. In addition, every such exercise contains particulars of two or more alternative courses of action and their expected financial outcomes. Whatever method of appraisal is used, it is expected that a conclusion will be reached of the kind "Course X is preferable (or preferred) to Course Y" or, in other words, "Course X is worth more than Course Y."

Now suppose that a firm has \$10,000 in cash and has two courses of action open to it, X of which the net present value is \$12,000, and Y of which the net present value is \$11,000. We would not, at the date in question, say that the firm had a greater cash balance than \$10,000. Suppose next that the firm has not \$10,000 in cash but an asset A which has a resale price of \$10,000. And suppose that course X is to sell the asset A and use the proceeds otherwise, and course Y is to continue to use the asset. And suppose the net present values of X and Y are as before. As in the previous case, course X is worth more than course Y.

But it would be just as useless in this case to show the asset A in an amount different from $10,000 as it would be to show the cash in the previous case in an amount different from $10,000.

But suppose the *book value* of the present asset A is $8000 and that that is the only information known. If this were taken to be the limit of the financial capacity of the venture, course X could not even be considered. But if it were possible to borrow another $2000 and the borrowing of this was taken into account in assessing course X, the net present value of course X would be loaded with an additional $2000 initial outlay plus the interest charges—all quite improperly, since the (undisclosed) resale price is sufficient to make course X possible.

The example shows several things. First, we need to know the cash we have, or the cash equivalent of the cash and other things we have, if we are to do any calculating in respect of future alternatives. If we do not know this, our choices between alternatives will be mistaken; indeed, some feasible alternatives we may not even consider. And, as every judgment of relative worth is based on present facts and *expected* financial outcomes given the present facts, the only presently verifiable element in the calculations and the only uniformly used component of the calculations is the cash equivalent (or sum of the resale prices) of the assets.

The stockholders and the managers of companies are both faced with problems of the above kind: managers with choices between projects, stockholders with choices between companies (or, more generally still, between companies and other forms of investment). Now stockholders can discover day by day the cash equivalents of their present holdings and alternative stocks. What they need is something to inform their expectations of the financial outcomes of alternative investments on their part. As in the earlier example, it is impossible to form expectations of the performance of companies unless one knows how they are presently placed financially, that is to say, what they own and in what proportions the equities in those assets run to different classes of equity holder. But stockholders cannot be expected to form any idea of the inflows and outflows from the specific operations of the many firms in which they may invest. They can, however, be informed of the effectiveness of the *whole* of the past operations of companies and their managements; they are so informed by the rates at which the equities of residual equity holders have been increased. These, the achieved rates of return of companies, may be modified by actual or prospective investors when forming their expectations, in the light of their views on the expected impact of general or specific trade conditions. The process is exactly analogous to the formation of managerial expectations, even though the calculations are of a less specific kind. But none of these calculations or expectations can be serviceable unless it is based on financial statements expressing positions and results in contemporary, and therefore comparable, terms.[5]

There are, of course, some who hold that, when a set of assets and equities is put together, we have something greater than the sum of the parts. It is implied that the aggregation of the cash equivalents of assets represents, if anything, less than the whole firm. Of course this is true. The whole firm in its concrete manifestation, however, is not what balance sheets represent. They represent in some sense the amount of the investment in assets and the apportionment of that amount among the classes of equity holders. It is true that any given collection of assets may be put together in different ways by different managers of them. But the effect of putting them together and to work in a given way is the net income yielded, year by year. When we know the amounts and composition of the assets and equities of any firm and what it produces (in financial terms) from time to time, we have all that is necessary to describe it and with what effect it has been managed. We can compare these characteristics with like characteristics of any other company, and with any more general form of investment; on the basis of knowledge of the past and present and of *general* expectations of the future, we may formulate specific expectations in respect of future possibilities for as many alternatives as we choose to consider.

In much of the literature the kinds of comparison we have been mentioning seem to be regarded as occasional or unusual. For example, the arguments against uniformity in accounting and the arguments for diversity with specification of the methods used give scant regard to the conditions under which comparison is possible. They are, in this respect, quite at odds with the reflective exercises which are part of judging and choosing. We cannot judge anything without some other past or present thing in mind. We do not choose unless we have at least two possible things in mind. Far from being unusual, comparison is of the essence in judging and choosing. And judging and choosing are potentially everyday exercises. But we cannot judge, choose, or compare commercial propositions in terms of all their specific differences by reference only to financial statements. We use financial statements

5. The argument is presented in more elaborate form in "Measures and Values," *The Accounting Review* (Apr. 1968).

to inform us only of financial elements of judgments and choices. However, in respect to their commercial outcomes, whatever specific nonfinancial elements we may want to consider, we cannot judge or choose unless we can reduce all the financial facts to common order—equally up-to-date and equally inclusive of the effects of past decisions and of the impact of past events of the nondecided kind.

It is vain to pretend that the prices of things have not risen when in fact they have. It is vain to contend that these changes are immaterial and that their consequences should be omitted from accounts. It is vain to pretend that the purchasing power of money has not risen or fallen when in fact it has. It is vain to expect managers or outsiders to be able to take cognizance, in their reflections, of the specific effects of these changes on particular firms and their results. For it is quite possible that, for any common class of assets, the prices of the holdings of one company may move at a different rate from, and even in opposite direction to, the prices of the holdings of another company. And it is quite possible that the different asset compositions of two companies will expose them quite differently to the effects of changes in the purchasing power of money.

It is also vain to attempt to exclude or separately to identify the effects of these different kinds of change. It is widely said that some of these effects are controllable, or at least are subject to managerial choice, while others are not. In simple thought experiments it is possible to isolate all kinds of possible variation. But in the complex of commercial operations of any firm, any kind of variation is intimately associated with other kinds. And few are strictly controllable. If the *C* company sold $1 million worth of goods in one year and planned to sell the same in the next year, and yet only half of its customers placed orders in the next year, it cannot be said that sales were, in any worthwhile sense, controllable by its managers. The risks of business are that fashions will change, wants will change, techniques will change, personnel will change, prices will change, the purchasing power of money will change. It is unrealistic to suppose that managers can cope with, make provision against, or respond to some of these changes and not others. And there are so many ways in which they can respond that the only safe way to treat the effects of these changes is to capture them all as well as is possible.[6]

6. Arguments against the separate identification of elements of the increment in residual equity are given at several points in *Accounting, Evaluation, and Economic Behavior*, pp. 118–19, 226–27, 236–37.

It seems unnecessary to illustrate further the particular ways in which present knowledge bears on judgments of the past and expectations of the future. The present is the link between past and future. Present financial position is the link between past events and future events. If it is not known, we cannot knowledgeably review the past or plan for the future. The past and present are in principle knowable and unalterable; the future is not knowable, but we can guess, calculate, and plan its shape if we know what the past has yielded and how we stand presently. These distinctions between past, present, and future have been the basis of much of my own work. I can readily admit the necessity of future calculations; but I cannot see how those calculations can be made or, if made, can be worthwhile without the fullest possible knowledge of the present financial state of a firm and the fullest possible account of its past.

Some Contrasts

The method of analysis we have illustrated proceeds from particular kinds of problem situations to which any person or firm may be exposed. It may well be asked in what way this method differs from the methods of others who have advanced proposals different from our own. The difference lies in the particularity with which we examined the situations we described and with which we could have examined other such problem situations. Lest it be supposed that this is not a material difference in method, it will be instructive to look at the methods used in developing some other proposed bodies of principles. It will be found that, in general, the authors of these proposals do not go back to the specific commercial settings in which financial information is used; their method is to expound or to reformulate ideas which are held or debated *among accountants*. It is as if the proof of the pudding were in the mixing, not in the eating.

Moonitz' study *The Basic Postulates of Accounting*, as indeed other studies to be mentioned, has a specific professional and temporal setting. It will be recalled that the work of the reconstituted Research Division of the AICPA was viewed as a potential corrective of the piecemeal examination of professional problems over the previous two decades. The antecedent research bulletins addressed themselves to accounting technicalities, however, not to the utility of the resulting information. The connections between information and its use were never established. Had they been established, it would perhaps have been sufficient, in the postulates study, to deal with the users and uses of accounting information in summary fashion and to pass on to the terms of art, which are at least one stage removed from commercial calculation and dealing. The Moonitz study concerns itself principally with these terms of art—the particular constructs and language forms common in debates among accountants. There will not be found in the study any illustration of the precise way in which accounting information enters into the processes of choice or judgment, although examples of certain kinds of decision are named (e.g., pp. 28–29) and decision-making is elsewhere referred to in less specific terms (e.g., p. 27).

We are not here concerned with the merits of the discussion in the study of such terms of art as "assets," "entities," "accounting periods," "going concerns," and so on. We are simply pointing out that, in the absence of proven connections between choices and certain antecedent financial information, the discussion of higher-level abstractions is premature. We choose only one example of the effect of the absence of explicit and admitted connection. We are told that, "without statements of position we have no starting point, no end, no check points to verify our measures of change" (p. 16). Then later: "For the most part, accounting data rely on *past* prices, but not entirely. Pressures have been building up in recent years for more use of future, and hence estimated, events and prices in order to make accounting reports 'more useful' "; it is suggested that nothing "stands in the way of such a development" (p. 29). The two stated views are, of course, inconsistent. Analysis of the particular elements of any financial or quasi-financial problem would have suggested that complete *information* on past events and present position and future *estimates* based on present position are *both* essential in choosing and that the mixing of past and future, of events and expectations, in reports of one kind (as the second quoted passage suggests), cannot serve to inform choices.

The Illinois study, *A Statement of Basic Accounting Postulates and Principles*, makes no direct reference to specific uses or users of accounting information. There are, of course, references to stewardship (pp. 2, 3), to "maximization of the benefits of resource utilization" (pp. 2, 3), to "decisions to be made by the various interests in an enterprise" (p. 3), and to serving "the needs of a variety of interests . . . whose needs vary" (p. 15). Notice that the components of all these phrases are abstractions, or constructs. None refers to such specific details as concern any person or persons engaged in trade or persons having to consider the merits of alternative courses of action. The whole discourse is lifted away from the context of the marketplace. We do not claim that discourse in general terms or by recourse to constructs is improper. We do claim, however, that in the absence of examples of the particular uses of the information generated by any process we are given no ground for supposing that one kind of accounting is any better than any other; what is more to the point, we have no ground for supposing that any particular kind of accounting is of any use at all.

True, the statement has a section on transactions. But nowhere are we given the anatomy or mechanics of the reflective process which precedes transactions, nor of the parts played by various kinds of financial magnitude and calculation in that process. True, we are told that "accounting fulfils a social need by reporting data which provide a basis for evaluating the success with which enterprise management has utilized the scarce resources entrusted to it" (p. 32). But nowhere are we given a single illustration of an evaluative device used by society or by individuals.

The AAA statement, ASOBAT, is much more specific in dealing with the actual or potential users of accounting information than the Moonitz study and the Illinois statement. There are statements of the kinds of decision which are made by named classes of parties—investors, suppliers, creditors, employees, and others (p. 21). But nowhere is there a suggestion of the ways in which particular pieces of financial information enter into those decisions and choices. We are told specifically that information on earnings, financial position, and liquidity is necessary (pp. 23–25). But we are treated to no discussion of the variant meanings of these terms and no particular definition or analysis of any one of them. Indeed, most of the discussion is devoted to the prediction of future earnings, positions, and cash-flows without any ostensible connection between specific present knowledge and specific estimations or predictions.

There are occasional pieces of evidence or occasional dicta which may be taken as indicating the futility of some kinds of accounting. Thus historical cost accounting is said to lead to undervaluation of assets and overstatement of earnings following inflation (p. 28). It is alleged that accounting on the basis of "current values (however defined) fails to satisfy a number of [unspecified] uses" (p. 30). But there is no illustration of the ways in which the alleged defects would distort judgments or estimates in any specified commercial circumstance.

Perhaps our request for definition and specific illustration will be considered pedantic. But we may very well believe that to define and illustrate would be much too uncomfortable a task when the authors were committed to the parallel reporting of positions and results on *two* bases. Their conclusion inevitably means that earnings, working capital, net assets, owners' equity, rate of return, leverage ratio, and other such aggregates and relations can have two different magnitudes at the same time. But analysis of the particular uses which can be made of these magnitudes in commercial reckoning would show that their components could ideally be of one kind only.

As in other cases, the discussion is removed entirely from contact with the commercial choices which, because there is no other source of information of the same kind, accounting might be expected to inform. The greater part of the statement employs terms and phrases which relate to debates among accountants and notions peculiar to accountants. It does not come down to the level of the city's haggling, choosing, and economizing. Its propositions are not, therefore, based on explicit inferences from observables, and its conclusions are not submitted to the test of usefulness in identified problem-contexts.

Time and space prevent us from dealing here with other recent theoretical works and the textbooks which purport to deal with accounting as an aid to decision-making. Generally, their style is the same as the examples noticed above. Allusions to particular situations in which factual and hypothetical financial magnitudes and relationships are used are missing. There is no discussion of the commercial significance of asset-backing, achieved ratio of return, debt to equity ratios, indicators of liquidity—which among them embrace all the figures which appear in periodical financial statements. The reader is left to suppose that these things are of no account (a conclusion flatly contradicted by the literature and practice of security analysis); that, if they are of importance, the necessary figures must be obtained otherwise than from accounting statements (yet no indication is given in the literature of any systematic alternative source); or that the specific magnitudes of these indicators may be used without regard for the effects of the different accounting rules used by any firm, or as between firms, on the component elements of the indicators (which is patently false).

In the absence of this analysis, there is no foundation for conclusions by way of deductive inference. The occasional allusions to deduction, as a method of reaching conclusions, are generally pointless, for seldom are they followed by explicit application of the deductive process to any set of premises for the reaching of any stated conclusion; where a line of deductive argument *is* begun, it is dropped in mid-course, and attention is switched to more palatable assertions.[7]

Finally, there is no attempt to indicate how the magnitudes derivable by any proposed accounting process would eliminate specified defects of alternative processes or would positively advance the capacity for informed judgment of users of accounting statements. Seldom are there references to reported failures, misdemeanors, or disputes as evidence of the propriety or impropriety of any process or conception. The world of commerce is just disregarded, instead of being regarded as the laboratory in which proposals and theories are refined and put under test. It seems unlikely that progress will be made as long as accountants are content to find shelter under the idea that magnitudes and methods are matters of opinion and are content to disregard the confusion which stems from the coexistence of materially different conceptions of what matters in daily commercial experience.

An Analogy

The kinds of exercise we have described in the previous section arise from the belief that what accountants do provides the empirical foundation of principles and theories.[8] Given this belief, it is easy to understand the consequential belief that to proceed from observable practices to principles is to follow the same steps as other sciences follow. We hold that this is a mistaken view.

We may use an analogy from, say, chemistry. If we watch closely the things which a chemist does in a laboratory, we can report every step he takes. We can collect descriptions of what many chemists do—put measured quantities of solids and fluids of certain kinds into test tubes and retorts; observe their interaction in atmospheric air or under exposure to heat, and so on; and weigh or otherwise measure the products. None of these observations, however, would provide any knowledge at all of the laws, principles, or theories of chemistry. We could say it is generally accepted practice among chemists always to use clean instruments or containers, always to weigh or measure inputs

7. Examples are the switch in treatment between the first half and the second half of Canning's *The Economics of Accountancy*; the switch from exit prices, after making a strong case for their use, by Edwards and Bell (*The Theory and Measurement of Business Income*); and the switch from dual values to a single value in Ijiri's *The Foundations of Accounting Measurement.*

8. This belief is at least implicit in all attempts to provide a rationalization for existing practices.

and outputs in particular ways, and always to write down or otherwise record what they have done. But all this describes only the overt and superficial elements of what chemists do. Chemical knowledge subsists in statements of the ways in which chemical substances can be related to one another or mixed with one another, and with what effects. The routines of chemists are intended to insure that they do not draw false inferences from the reactions and other events they bring about and observe. But they are not the empirical foundations of chemical knowledge.

It is exactly the same in accounting. Knowledge of financial calculation subsists in statements of the ways in which specific kinds of financial magnitudes can be related to one another or mixed with one another, and with what effects. If we know the effects we wish to bring about—magnitudes which will inform others of what has happened, of how firms stand in financial relation to the rest of the community, of the present capacity for varied but unspecified actions at any time—we can devise routines which will bring about just those effects. The empirical foundations of accounting knowledge lie in the kinds of financial magnitudes which men find it necessary and reasonable to relate, add, subtract, and compare if certain kinds of judgments are to be made or certain kinds of conclusions are to be drawn in respect of commercial or financial matters. They do not lie in the kinds of practices accountants have become accustomed to following.

There seem to be grounds for supposing that the widely held dictum, that different kinds of information are necessary for different kinds of decision, also has its roots in the variant practices of accountants rather than in close examination of reflective processes. We may use another analogy. The properties of common salt are numerous. Its components are sodium and chlorine in a fixed proportion; its specific gravity is given by a fixed number; its molecular weight is a fixed number; its solubility is known; and the ways in which it combines with other chemicals are known. Any given user of sodium chloride in a chemical process may make use of knowledge of these properties in any combination, depending on what process he is concerned with and what he intends to produce. But it would be futile to expect to produce what he intends if specific gravity, molecular weight, solubility, and so on did not have unequivocal values.

It is exactly the same in the case of the financial properties of firms. If we know (1) the financial position of a firm at a given time, (2) the composition of its assets and equities, (3) the net income it has recently earned, we can put these pieces of information together in any way which is relevant to the kind of choice or judgment we may wish to make. If we happen to be investors, we can relate these magnitudes or any pertinent combination of them to their counterparts for other firms and other forms of investment and to the prices of other securities and investments, which we can discover independently of financial statements. But only if they are unequivocal magnitudes. If we happen to be managers, we can relate these magnitudes or any pertinent combination of them to the counterparts mentioned and to the prices of any other potential assets which we can discover, at any time, independently of the accounting process.

What is necessary for different kinds of decision is not, therefore, different kinds of information, but different combinations of the components of a body of information of the same kind. Investors as a class are not solely concerned with the magnitude of a year's income; some are concerned with the magnitude of net assets, some with the relationship between assets and equities. As the composition of some will change in the light of the firm's performance and external commercial events, it is necessary to provide the kind of information which is usable by all. Similarly creditors and financiers as a class are not concerned solely with asset coverage; some, at times, are concerned with net income and its components—but not a *different* net income or one calculated on different principles from the net income which is of interest to stockholders. Managers as a class are not solely concerned with any particular financial property of a firm, but with them all—and with such quantified expressions of those properties as will serve them in as many possible problem contexts as possible.

As we have said, we will not find the empirical foundations of accounting in the variant practices and conceptions of accountants. They will be found only from the widest survey of the potential uses of financial information in commercial reckoning and from the attempt to find just that kind of information which is commonly usable by all parties to commercial and financial dealings.

Conclusion

To devise and subsequently to test theories by reference to the phenomena they deal with is the normal and accepted course of all empirical science. We have aimed to illustrate the same processes in this paper. The phenomena in question are statements about the effects of particular transactions and other events which bear on the financial positions and results of firms. The questions at issue are: "What kinds of particular and aggregate statements are usable and necessary in the specific contexts of specific problem situations?" and "Of those kinds, which are worthwhile continuously recording and periodically reporting because they are parts of the ongoing history of the financial affairs of firms?"

We considered a number of typical problem situations which indicate that contemporary resale prices are pertinent to judgments of past results and choices based on present potentials at any time. We found no use or need for book-values which are inconsistent with market prices. We concluded that representations of the effects on a given firm of all its transactions, and of all changes in the prices of its assets, and of changes in the purchasing power of money, are necessary if those without immediate knowledge of acquaintance are not to be misinformed.

The types of transaction and event we discussed are factual in character, and the modes of reckoning and dealing considered we hold to be typical and verifiable. These constitute the core of factual premises for our conclusions. They are the real stuff of commerce. They must somehow be embraced by any theory of the generation of pertinent financial information.

Every theory makes use of some generalized terms, idealizations, or constructs. These are inventions. But if they are to be serviceable they must have demonstrable empirical correlates. It may be said that any theorist is entitled, is free, to choose his own constructs. But with that freedom runs the obligation to show how the constructs are related to observed and experienced events and to show how the products his theory entails engage with the reflections and actions of men in active commerce. There can be no useful construct in a theory of accounting which is not firmly tied, directly or indirectly, to some choice or action of a commercial kind. We noticed however that the literature generally fails to deal with observable events in their temporal and circumstantial settings and fails to consider the specific connections of the products of the theories propounded with the known criteria of choice in commercial matters.

I have not in this paper attempted to illustrate all the commercial situations in which statements of financial position based on resale prices, and statements of results embracing the effects of changes in prices and the purchasing power of money, are relevant. The general ideas of continuously contemporary accounting,[9] as I have expounded them elsewhere, have arisen from consideration of such situations. They have been supported by observation of commercial events, disputes, frauds, and failures, as well as by analysis of the notorious conflicts in the present body of doctrine.

The theory of continuously contemporary accounting takes cognizance of all the factors which have given rise to suggestions for different forms of accounting. It is more fully historical than historical cost accounting. It embraces the effects which price-level-adjusted accounting attempts to cope with. It embraces the effects which replacement-price accounting attempts to cope with. It is geared to the calculation of expected outcomes of future possibilities. Its products are capable of being related to any other financial magnitudes at a given time. Each of the types of accounting just mentioned has the recognition of some element of commercial reality as its justification. But each ignores some other aspects of that reality, and in that sense each falls short of the ideal system which would cope with all of the elements of commercial experience.

My object has been to suggest that the methods of empirical science have scarcely been tried in accounting. The common observables and experiences of commercial reckoning and dealing are generally disregarded; yet they are the only legitimate foundation for a viable theory and serviceable practices. In place of their analysis, we have discussions of higher-level abstractions, discussions which drift away from or point only vaguely in the direction of the very points of choice and judgment at which accounting information is used.

Whatever confidence I have in my own inference from these experiences and observables may be shaken by demonstration of their falsity. But I do not believe that any worthwhile theory of accounting or any worthwhile practice can emerge otherwise than from examination of the exigencies of men engaged in the calculating, choosing, and dealing characteristic of the marketplace.

9. I allude here to the main ideas mentioned in the previous sentence. Some of the suggestions made in *Accounting, Evaluation, and Economic Behavior* I would now modify, but only through stronger belief in the propriety of the main ideas. A paper on these modifications is forthcoming.

Are There Commercial Foundations of Accounting Theory?

Kermit D. Larson

THE TITLE of Professor Chambers' paper "The Commercial Foundations of Accounting Theory" suggests an attempt to explicate those commercial events, things, or characteristics which are believed to provide important premises in the development of accounting theory. Given Professor Chambers' stated opinion that "accounting is concerned strictly with commercial experiences, events, and considerations," the commercial foundations of accounting theory are seen to provide the empirical events which, if examined, dictate the commercially necessary information that should be generated by accounting. More particularly, the commercial foundations of accounting theory are "the common observables and experiences of commercial reckoning and dealing . . ."—"the exigencies of men engaged in the calculating, choosing, and dealing characteristic of the marketplace."

The main thrust of Chambers' paper involves a two-sided argument. On the one side, he argues that the general modes of inquiry and exposition in accounting fail to adequately comprehend the empirical foundations of accounting, which are the common observables and experiences of commercial reckoning and dealing. He states, "the literature generally fails to deal with observable events in their temporal and circumstantial settings and fails to consider the specific connections of the products of the theories propounded with the known criteria of choice in commercial matters." On the other side of the argument, it is asserted that the "current cash equivalent" theory of accounting is firmly grounded in these commercial foundations; the products of current cash equivalent accounting are deduced from the specific commercial settings in which financial information is used.

Establishing the Relevance of Accounting to Decisions

Perhaps the most critical issue raised in Chambers' paper is the general inability of accountants to clearly justify the data outputs of accounting by showing the significance of the data to specific decision-making processes. In my opinion, this problem is likely the most critical impediment to the improvement of accounting theory and practices. I generally agree with Professor Chambers that the recognition of this problem implies a criticism of the typical modes of inquiry found in accounting literature. All too often the analyses of alternative accounting procedures have included little or no consideration of the specific ways in which the resulting information might bear upon decision processes. Contrary to Chambers, however, I reject the argument that this deficiency is *essentially* a consequence of inadequate modes of inquiry and exposition. The whole process of assessing the relevance relationship between data and decision is a highly complex and problematical affair. To deny our general state of "ignorance of how people behave in commercial situations" and to assert that there are known criteria of choice in commercial matters constitutes, in my view, a simplistic perception of human decision. Indeed, the recent surge of interest in behavioral accounting research might be explained, in large part, as a direct response to the problem that the criteria of choice in commercial matters are not known.

Several problems in the analysis of human decision may impinge upon the process of determining what information is or is not relevant to a decision. Suppose, for example, a decision-maker develops an idealistic decision model, that is, a model which correctly incorporates all of the important factors such that employment of the model will maximize his objectives. Further, suppose that some of the important variables in the decision-maker's model are unknowable (perhaps because they will be determinant only in the future). A *possible* course of action is for the decision-maker to seek information regarding those variables which are knowable, make subjective estimations of those which are not, and continue to use the basic (idealized) model that is consistent with his overall objectives. A second course of action is equally possible, however. The entire model may be cast aside (due perhaps to the frustration which results from repeated answering of questions to which there are no answers). In its place there may be substituted a surrogate model, all or most of the variables of which are knowable. The analytical processes of the surrogate model may not even resemble those that were characteristic of the more idealistic model. This surrogate decision model is utilized because it is easy to employ, and the decision-maker reasonably presumes that the results of the model more or less crudely conform to those that would have been obtained using the idealistic model under idealistic conditions.

If the process of decision-making proceeds along the lines that I have outlined—and Chambers' analysis provides no evidence to contradict the employment of surrogate decision models—the accounting theorist is faced with special difficulties in establishing the relevance of accounting data to the decision. There is no clear understanding on the part of the decision-maker, or on the part of anyone else, as to the closeness of fit between the idealistic decision model and the surrogate decision model that the decision-maker actually uses. Further, the surrogate model, like any surrogate, is not deductible from the decision-maker's general objectives or from the form of the idealized model, even if these were knowable. Accountants may and should engage in expansive research regarding the decision-making function, one result of which might be to discover the extent to which surrogate decision models are actually used by decision-makers. Perhaps then accountants can determine the form of those models and can provide the necessary informational inputs. However, even this is not entirely satisfactory, for we must rest completely upon the decision-maker's ability to pick good surrogate models.

It is not the purpose of this discussion to provide an exhaustive list of the deficiencies in our knowledge of human decision-making. One further example may, however, enforce the argument that the criteria of choice in commercial matters are not in the least established by one man's opinions as to the ways in which decisions are actually made.

Some choice situations are such that all of the important criteria can be determined with reasonable accuracy. In such cases, the act of choice is not so much a matter of decision as it is mechanical calculation. In many other choice situations, *some* of the critical criteria are not capable of verifiable measurement. In the latter event, the decision-maker may not even be able to perceive an idealized model—a model that would be applicable if the important criteria were susceptible to verifiable measurement. This state might result from a highly ambiguous set of fact conditions in which the parameters of each alternative are poorly structured and subject to great uncertainty. In simpler terms, the decision-maker recognizes that a choice must be made and knows little more than that he is faced with a very vague and poorly structured problem. Under these conditions, even the isolation of a surrogate decision model may be of questionable validity. *Ex ante*, the decision-maker simply decides to "sleep on it" and then chooses. *Ex post*, the decision model uncovered by a researcher or the decision-maker is likely to reflect much more a rationalization of the actual choice than it is to reflect the criteria that played a significant role in the decision.

To whatever extent accounting assists in reaching decisions of this sort, the relevance of accounting data can only be presumed. I do not argue that these limitations of accounting represent insurmountable barriers to the future development of accounting. I do argue, however, that, given our present state of ignorance regarding the criteria of choice in commercial situations, the present relevance of accounting data under current cash equivalent accounting, or any other form, must ultimately be presumed.

The Role of Opinion

The previous comments and what will follow consist in large part of my personal opinions on the subject matter and nature of accounting theory. Correspondingly, it is appropriate that we consider Professor Chambers' beliefs regarding the role of opinion. In proposing to explicate the failure to develop any clear lines of thought on accounting theory during the last decade, Chambers argues that two particular aspects of the modes of inquiry and exposition in accounting have been causal. First is the noticeable reluctance to assign definite and limited functions to accounting. Second, "Almost everyone seems to think that he is entitled to an opinion on the subject matter and the nature of accounting theory—an opinion, what is more, which others will respect. . . . However, there can be no more mischievous idea than that the choice of the magnitudes recorded and reported and the choice of rules of processing are matters of opinion. There can be no greater source of disruption and confusion. For if these things are matters of opinion, there can be no solid core of principles, no ascertainable function, no systematic knowledge. It should be well known that it is profitless to debate matters of opinion."

Perhaps the entire argument against opinion is an attempt to refute the long-established method of, what I would call, reasoning by authority. This procedure is clearly evident in some of the widely read classics of accounting, in which the conclusions are supported not so much by an appeal to logic as by the authoritative style of presenting the author's opinions. Nevertheless, the pitfalls of this tradition can certainly be renounced without adopting the naive approach of purging opinion from the process of determining accounting procedures. It is not profitless to debate matters of opinion; to argue otherwise is to refute the possibility that opinions take cognizance of experience or facts. It is to deny that opinions may provide partial strains of reasoning where no complete logical patterns exist. Finally, it fails to accept the existing state of affairs in accounting, wherein decisions as to the magnitudes recorded and reported and the choice of rules of processing must be made today and wherein countless alternatives exist between which choice is necessarily a matter of opinion.

I have previously noted Chambers' criticism of the "noticeable reluctance to assign definite and limited functions to accounting." Obviously, the assigned functions of accounting have a direct impact on the choice of the magnitudes to be recorded and the rules of processing. I might point out that the functions which Chambers assigns to accounting are supported by nothing more than his opinion. And this is as it should be, for the normative theorist's assignment of functions is necessarily a matter of opinion.

The Significance and Meaning of Present Position

The argument of Chambers' paper, consistent with his previous work, makes a sharp distinction between past, present, and future and places a special importance upon the definition and measurement of present position. It is in large part this special emphasis on the present vis-à-vis the future that distinguishes Chambers' work from that of many other contemporary writers. He states: "Present financial position is the link between past events and future events. If it is not known, we cannot knowledgeably review the past or plan for the future. The past and present are in principle knowable and unalterable; the future is not knowable.... We hold this process of discovery [of what has occurred and of the resulting present position] to be the prime function of accounting. If it is not done as well as is possible, judgments about past and future lack that contact with the factual present which alone provides a trustworthy foundation for choice and action."

There are at least three reasons cited in support of the relative emphasis placed upon calculations which relate to the present. Each of these three arguments which underlie the attributed significance of present position in accounting is worthy of further consideration.

THE CAPACITY TO ACT—AN ATTRIBUTE OF THE PRESENT

The first reason for the relative significance of the present is that the process of choosing between alternative courses of action necessarily depends upon the capacity to engage in future action. If the decision is to be made in the present or the near future, the capacity of importance is *present capacity*. Thus, the attribute of the present which is of special importance to choice in commercial affairs, and therefore of importance to accounting, is the capacity to engage in commercial action.

Clearly, the capacity to act is an important factor in the selection and evaluation of alternative courses of action. Unless one considers and evaluates alternatives in light of his capacity to act, feasible alternatives may be inappropriately excluded from consideration, and nonfeasible alternatives may be inappropriately included in the evaluation.[1]

Narrowing the analysis to accounting statements of financial position, Chambers points out that the present capacity of stockholders is, of course, discoverable by reference to the marketplace rather than to the firm's statement of financial position. We may note that this point should be generalized to include the capacities of *all external* parties. The present capacities of external parties to take market action obviously are not portrayed by a firm's statement of financial position. This is true regardless of the class of external party one may wish to consider, e.g., investors, suppliers, customers. Thus, to the extent that information regarding the present is used to determine present capacity of the actor, which usage is distinguished from the possible significance of present information as a basis for predicting the future, the statement of financial position must be relevant only to decisions made on behalf of the entity.

Other critics have addressed themselves to the problem of determin-

1. It must be emphasized that the analysis of this section is not concerned with the possible significance of present capacity as a basis for estimating future results of a course of action. That point will be covered subsequently.

ing the particular managerial decision situations in which a statement of financial position, prepared to reflect exit prices, would be relevant and those situations in which it may not be relevant. I wish to raise the far more general problem of the great presumptive gap that exists between a statement of financial position—that is, a report which is defined in terms of the accounting procedures that are employed in the statement's construction—and a concept of financial position—which purports to specify the informational significance of the concept. In other words, it is one thing to define the term "financial position" as the present capacity of a firm to engage in future market action. It is quite a different thing to define financial position as a classified array of a firm's assets and equities, measured in terms of their current cash equivalents (or any other type of measurement for that matter). These two approaches to the definition of financial position result in a matching pair of concepts, the correspondence of which can only be presumed, given our present state of analytical refinement.

Does Chambers' statement of financial position adequately portray the capacity of a firm to engage in future market actions? However this question is answered, the answer will incorporate to a significant extent the personal opinions of the respondent. An affirmative answer will be less discomforting if one is willing to exclude from consideration the elements of present financial capacity which are executory, such as the capacity to issue additional stock. Similarly, one's confidence in the descriptive validity of this statement of financial position will be buoyed if the present capacity to engage in future market actions is somehow perceived as being separate and distinct from the current cash equivalents associated with packaging the firm's assets in various alternative combinations. At the least, these factors would seem to cast serious doubt on the informational significance of Chambers' statement of financial position.

There is another general problem that creates great uneasiness in my mind regarding the informational significance of the statement of financial position. We all recognize that the present state of a firm is multidimensional in character. If I abstract from the present state of the firm those characteristics which pertain to its capacity to engage in future financial activities, I am still left with a large multidimensional set of characteristics. Such factors as the existing state of managerial talent and the degree of flexibility and skill evidenced by the firm's labor force would seem to be important elements of consideration in assessing the firm's present capacity to engage in future financial activities. But these characteristics are not described in the statement of financial position. Giving adequate recognition to the awesome complexity of a large corporation's present position, the representation of present capacity is, perhaps, entirely too lofty an objective to hold for the balance sheet.

FINANCIAL POSITION—A BASIS FOR ESTIMATING THE FUTURE

A second reason for the special significance attributed to the present is that knowledge of the present position, and of the past, is viewed as providing the major factual premises for speculation about the future. Chambers states: "it is impossible to form expectations of the performance of the companies unless one knows how they are presently placed, financially. . . . I can readily admit the necessity of future calculations; but I cannot see how those calculations can be made, or if made can be worthwhile, without the fullest possible knowledge of the present financial state of a firm and the fullest possible account of its past."

In the previous section the statement of financial position was discussed in terms of its purported representation of the capacity to act. Financial position in that sense was noted to be of significance only to parties acting on behalf of the firm. To the contrary, when financial position is analyzed as the factual basis which underlies estimations of the future, the statement of financial position is seen to have potential informational significance to all parties (internal and external). All parties considering future actions related to a firm will be interested in information that is serviceable in predicting or estimating what the future holds for the firm. It should be re-emphasized that retrospective and contemporary calculations in accounting are of no significance to external parties unless they aid in the process of making predictions.

Unfortunately, except for a few rather strongly worded statements to the effect that future expectations *must* be based upon present and past financial information, scant attention is given to the specific ways in which contemporary and historical financial information is serviceable in predicting the future. This would seem to be a natural result of the view that the future is in principle unknowable, and that "all the results and inferences from [future calculations] are individual and subjective."[2]

The problems of future estimation that are faced by stockholders

2. Raymond J. Chambers, *Accounting, Evaluation, and Economic Behavior* (Englewood Cliffs, N.J.: Prentice-Hall, 1966), p. 84.

were treated only by an analogy. The supposedly analogous example was of a firm which owned one asset and had two investment alternatives. However, in that example the net present value of each alternative was given as part of the facts of the example. Thus, the example had nothing to do with the problems of estimating the future with regard to each alternative. Correspondingly, it is essentially irrelevant to the stockholder's problem. It certainly does not show the specific ways in which financial statement information should be used to predict the future consequences that will result from an investment in stock.

It is indisputable that predictions of the future are dependent upon our knowledge of past events and present conditions. But the events and characteristics of the past and the present are generally complex, frequently multidimensional, and always unbounded in number. Some process of selecting certain events and characteristics for analysis, and omitting others, is obviously necessary. Chambers' belief that future calculations cannot be made in a worthwhile manner "without the fullest possible knowledge of the present financial state of a firm and the fullest possible account of its past" begs the question and obscures the basic problems of deciding which events and characteristics should be included in the descriptive scheme of accounting and which should be excluded. There are many approaches to estimating what the future holds for a firm, and I would venture that a significant proportion of them involve minimal consideration of balance-sheet information, whether or not exit prices are used as the basis of preparation. I know of no way to specify the relevance of retrospective and contemporary calculations to prediction other than to carefully examine the predictive process and to show precisely how and under what caveats certain kinds of historical data can be incorporated into a specified predictive model.

THE NEED FOR VERIFICATION

A third reason supporting the pre-eminent position of the present in accounting is that, contrary to anticipatory calculations of the future, the present (and the past) is, in principle, knowable. Thus, if accounting is constrained by the objective of providing information which is factual—which is susceptible to present verification—it must be constrained to exclude anticipatory calculations.

In appreciation of the inherent risk associated with making predictions, many accountants may accept, on practical grounds, the exclusion of anticipatory calculations from the domain of accounting. As a theoretical matter, however, the relative emphasis on the present and the past and the corresponding exclusion of anticipatory calculations from the domain of accounting are suspect. The descriptive or explanatory objectives of accounting are, in my view, wholly analogous to the objectives of other empirical sciences in which predictive capacity is a widely recognized objective. The inability to presently verify predictions of the future need not be considered an insurmountable hurdle. The theoretical utility of independent corroboration relates to the verification of the predictive process, not to the specific instance of prediction.

These arguments are supported by the interface between the predictive models of operations research and accounting. A more comprehensive view of the information-generating process in business firms —which would encompass both of these areas—would recognize anticipatory calculations as an integral part of that process.

Commercial Foundations—The Problem of Evidence

Professor Chambers argues that a viable theory of accounting for business firms must be grounded in the realities of commercial experience. More particularly, this involves explicating the specific ways in which the products of a theory are important elements in the evaluative and calculative processes underlying commercial decisions.

In support of his theory, Chambers provides illustrations which purport to state the important elements of consideration in certain commercial situations. I previously criticized one of those illustrations. It will be beneficial to consider the other illustration, for the purpose of supporting my argument that hypothetical examples are not evidence. Examples may provide a convenient mode of expressing one's opinion, but they do not provide evidence to substantiate the claim that the current cash equivalent theory of accounting is well grounded in the specific commercial settings in which financial information is used.

Chambers states: "[Firms] may pledge assets, singly or in total, as security for cash advances. The immediate security for lenders is the market selling price of the assets pledged. It is often said that the significant value of an asset to a firm is its calculated net present value in its present use. But no lender on the security of the firm's assets is concerned with the value of those assets to the firm in this sense. He is concerned with the value of those assets as generators of cash for himself in the event that he must enforce his claim against the borrower by sale of the charged asset." Consider an alternative view. Regarding the preponderance of debt financing in a highly industrialized economy, the market selling price of the assets pledged is, at best, of secondary significance to the lender. To the contrary, the primary element of significance is the firm's expected ability to service the debt, which is a function of the expected cash flows from the firm's operations and the degree of risk that corresponds to these expectations. Regarding those large firms which provide the vast majority of economic production in the United States and which engage in the vast majority of debt financing, liquidation is an extremely rare occurrence even in the case in which the firm is in financial distress. Further, few loan officers would grant credit if default were deemed a significant possibility.

Chambers continues the illustration: "Wherever a charge over particular assets or groups of assets is given as security for borrowings, there will be found some provision restricting other borrowing by reference to the amount of the assets of the borrower. Now the term 'the amount of the assets' in such an indenture can have only one kind of meaning. The object of the provision is to cover the amount borrowed. This cover is given, not by the book values of assets, however determined, but by the market values of assets." Consider an alternative view. When a lender requires that restrictions be placed upon other borrowing, the primary intent is to protect the ability of the firm to service the debt. If the restriction is stated by reference to an "amount of assets," that term is essentially a convenient and conventional surrogate for debt service capacity. Thus, the market values of the assets are generally of nominal significance in the sense of serving as a basis for predicting the results of liquidation.

I do not offer these alternative views as evidence of identified criteria of choice in commercial situations, albeit I submit they comprise a reasonable interpretation. I offer them only as an arguable point of view, for the purpose of rejecting such illustrations as adequate evidence to substantiate the commercial foundations of any accounting theory. Whatever lack of confidence I have in Chambers' inferences from his experiences and observations may be shaken by a demonstration of their empirical validity.

A Concluding Note

Are there commercial foundations of accounting theory? An affirmative answer follows directly from the perception that a primary function of accounting is to provide relevant information to persons making decisions which relate to market actions. Professor Chambers has clearly and forcefully argued that the criteria of choice in commercial affairs are an absolutely essential consideration in the development of accounting theory. The significance of this argument cannot be overemphasized.

The Balance Sheet—Embodiment of the Most Fundamental Elements of Accounting Theory

Robert T. Sprouse

THE ASSERTION is frequently made that in accounting's house the income statement is our most important product. To the extent that this is intended to mean that the attention of most users of financial statements tends to focus on the income statement, the assertion is acceptable. To the extent that the assertion refers to the most important elements of accounting theory, the assertion is delusory. This paper is written in support of an alternative proposition: the balance sheet embodies the most fundamental elements of accounting theory, from which the essential elements contained in the income statement are necessarily derived. Indeed, the income statement can properly be described as merely a summary of one class of transactions resulting in changes in one balance-sheet account.

I offer two forms of support for this proposition: (1) An analysis of two contending views of the components and function of the balance sheet that have emerged over time. The purpose is to demonstrate the fallacies and futilities of such opposing views. For convenience, let me designate these the sheet of balances view and the static funds statement view. (2) A positive case for reviewing the balance sheet as a statement of financial position which provides a basis for the measurement of a meaningful concept of income and which, at the same time, provides useful information in its own right. Each of these three distinguishable views has strikingly different implications for the construction of accounting theory—implications that are readily discernible in their application to the analysis of transactions and financial reporting.

THE SHEET OF BALANCES VIEW

The sheet of balances approach views the statement as a summary of debit and credit account balances that remain after the determinants of income have been decided upon and the retained earnings account has been adjusted for the amount of income that results. This is a "balance sheet" in the most literal sense of the term. Increasingly, this view has been adopted in accounting practice, as manifested by many of the pronouncements of the AICPA and by most of the financial statements published by corporations.

Accounting Terminology Bulletin no. 1 defines the balance sheet as "a tabular statement or summary of balances (debit and credit) carried forward after an actual or constructive closing of books of account kept according to principles of accounting."[1] An asset is "something represented by a debit balance that is or would be properly carried forward upon a closing of books of account according to the rules or principles of accounting."[2] Similarly, a liability is "something represented by a credit balance that is or would be properly carried forward upon a closing of books of account according to the rules or principles of accounting."[3]

Exaggerating only slightly, then, one might say that, according to this view, a balance sheet is a summary of debit and credit balances and that the primary difference between an asset and liability is the side of the account on which the balance happens to appear.

The sheet of balances view of the balance sheet stems from the notion that a valid and viable framework for accounting analysis—that is, an accounting theory—can be constructed on the basis of the pre-eminence of the income statement and the application of the "matching" concept. Which of these two—the pre-eminence of the income statement and the matching concept—is the chicken and which is the egg is difficult to determine. One might hypothesize that because both

1. AICPA, Committee on Terminology, *Review and Resume*, Accounting Terminology Bulletin no. 1 (New York, 1953), p. 12.
2. Accounting Terminology Bulletin no. 1, p. 13.
3. Accounting Terminology Bulletin no. 1, pp. 13–14.

are sterile—at least as foundations for accounting theory—they were necessarily created simultaneously.[4]

Pre-eminence of the income statement is the offspring of confusion between the derivative information that decision-makers may find most useful and the fundamental elements of a framework for accounting analysis from which that useful information is derived. More about that later. First let me elaborate on the sterility of the matching concept as an element of accounting theory.

Without pretending to have traced its historical origin, it seems safe to say that the matching concept first began to receive widespread attention with the publication of *An Introduction to Corporate Accounting Standards*[5] by Paton and Littleton. There, as one of the basic concepts that constitute a suitable foundation for accounting standards, the authors cited the matching of effort and accomplishment. The economic concept of income as a change in wealth during a period of time was explicitly rejected, even as an ideal, and the notion of an income associated with each item of goods sold or service rendered was expounded. The authors stated that "if this conception could be effectively realized in practice, the net accomplishment of the enterprise could be measured in terms of units of output rather than of intervals of time. . . . Time periods are a convenience, a substitute, but the fundamental concept is unchanged. The ideal is to match costs incurred with the effects attributable to or significantly related to such costs."[6]

The implications of this approach become particularly vivid with the following statements: "Accrual and deferment are closely related phases of the process of matching. The full accrual of labor cost, under the terms of the various contracts in effect, needs to be recog-

4. Delmer P. Hylton comments on the concurrent ascendancy of the income statement and "the accounting convention known as 'matching revenue with expense' " in "On Matching Revenue with Expense," *The Accounting Review* (Oct. 1965), pp. 824–28.

5. W. A. Paton and A. C. Littleton, *An Introduction to Corporate Accounting Standards* (Evanston, Ill.: AAA, 1940).

6. Paton and Littleton, p. 15. The AAA's 1964 Concepts and Standards Research Study Committee—The Matching Concept adopted some of the same language (e.g., "costs constitute a measure of business effort, and revenues represent accomplishments coming from those efforts") and concluded "that it is desirable to emphasize the matching concept in financial reporting." The committee meticulously avoided any reference to assets and liabilities although at times it appears to have been a strain (e.g., losses are viewed as "product or service factors given up in return for a zero quantity of revenue"). "The Matching Concept," *The Accounting Review* (Apr. 1965), pp. 368–72.

nized; otherwise the amount of labor-service received is incorrectly expressed. It is perhaps of secondary importance that wages earned but unpaid are recorded as part of the process. Deferred charges, broadly defined to include most assets, need to be recognized; otherwise the goods furnished or services rendered currently will be loaded with charges not significantly applicable. The flow of cost factors, in other words, needs to be appropriately divided between the pool of charges to be held back, deferred, and those representing elements from which the utility has been fully exhausted. Assets accrued but as yet uncollected should be recognized because, if they are ignored, services rendered will be incorrectly expressed."[7]

Note the relegation of the balance sheet to a sheet of balances created as a by-product of the matching process so that costs will not be incorrectly expressed. Although the deferred charges may include most assets, the objective is to avoid matching revenues with charges that are not significantly applicable and allow costs to be appropriately divided between deferred charges and expenses. This approach places a premium on judgment as to whether a cost is significantly applicable or inapplicable to a revenue and whether a division of a cost into amounts to be deferred and amounts to be expended is appropriate or inappropriate. Presumably, the matching process does not even require a concept of income to serve as a basis for making those judgments. Instead, as suggested by some: "Time is what we measure with a watch. Income is what we measure with a profit and loss statement."[8]

Inevitably, of course, it is recognized that, even if it were conceptually desirable, in most cases the matching of costs and revenues is a practical impossibility. In practice, most costs are identified with a period of time in much the same way that even proponents of the matching concept identify revenues with a period of time. Nevertheless, the matching concept, based as it is on the pre-eminence of the income statement and relying heavily on subjective notions of correctness, applicability, and propriety, is responsible for those unique accounting products that one so frequently finds in today's sheet of balances: deferred charges that are not assets and deferred credits that are not liabilities.

In its Opinion 11, "Accounting for Income Taxes," the APB cited certain general concepts and assumptions as relevant in considering

7. Paton and Littleton, p. 16.

8. John C. Burton, ed., *Corporate Financial Reporting: Conflicts and Challenges* (New York: AICPA, 1969), pp. 49–50, 225.

that problem. Among them, matching was recognized as one of the basic processes of income determination. The inherent sterility of the matching concept as a basis for resolving accounting issues is especially glaring, however, in the board's tautologous explanation that "expenses of the current period consist of those costs which are identified with the revenues of the current period and those costs which are identified with the current period on some basis other than revenue."[9]

Nevertheless, in rejecting the liability method, in rejecting the net of tax method, and in adopting the deferral method of interperiod tax allocation, the board stated explicitly that the "measurement of income tax expense becomes thereby a consistent and integral part of the *process of matching revenues and expenses* in the determination of results of operations."[10] In so doing, the board acknowledged that "deferred charges and deferred credits relating to timing differences represent the cumulative recognition given to their tax effects and as such do not represent receivables or payables in the usual sense."[11]

Elevated to "one of the most important principles in income determination"[12] and uninhibited by any meaningful concepts of assets, liabilities, and income, the matching concept may be deemed to supply adequate support for virtually any accounting procedure. As one author puts it: "In the minds of many accountants, this single convention outweighs all others; in other words, if a given procedure can be asserted to conform to the matching concept, nothing else need be said; the matter is settled and the procedure is justified."[13]

Obviously, the sheet of balances approach is operational; its everyday use is very much in evidence. At opposite extremes, however, this approach either permits maximum latitude in deciding which balances to carry forward, or it requires an ever increasing list of detailed rules and procedures to be promulgated designating which balances may properly be carried forward.

When new accounting problems arise—like the investment credit—this approach either allows a variety of individual decisions to be made or requires that some recognized authority such as the APB designate by vote what is the best rule or procedure. The process is much like

9. "Accounting for Income Taxes," APB Opinion 11 (New York: AICPA, Dec. 1967), p. 160.

10. APB Opinion 11, p. 169.

11. APB Opinion 11, p. 178.

12. Paul Grady, *Inventory of Generally Accepted Accounting Principles for Business Enterprises*, ARS 7 (New York: AICPA, 1965), p. 74.

13. Hylton, p. 824.

that of judges in a beauty contest where a winner is designated by vote based primarily on personal preference, there being no established concepts in determining beauty and in determining proper matching.

In keeping with democratic principles, the majority of such a group might "conclude that the allowable investment credit should be reflected in net income over the productive life of acquired property and not in the year in which it is placed in service,"[14] while the majority of another equally intelligent and experienced group might well conclude exactly the opposite.

One might ordinarily expect that an explicit concept of net income would be prerequisite to deciding what should be included in its measurement and what should not be included in its measurement. But, to my knowledge, no one has ever successfully managed to formulate a concept of income that is not directly or indirectly dependent upon the concept of assets and the concept of liabilities. It follows that the concepts of assets and liabilities are more fundamental than the concept of income. If this is the case, equal acceptability of three different methods of carrying forward deferred investment tax credit balances cannot be rationalized.[15]

In addition to the deferral method of accounting for the tax allocation and the deferral method of accounting for the investment credit, the matching concept and the sheet of balances view are responsible for a variety of other balance-sheet anomalies. Unamortized bond discount, unamortized discount, issue cost, redemption premium on bonds refunded, and the LIFO method of inventory valuation are a few that are sometimes found among assets. Deferred gain on sale and leaseback, equity in net assets of subsidiary over cost, provision for replacement of LIFO inventories, and reserve for decline in conversion value of Canadian assets are examples of reported liabilities.

In summary, the sheet of balances approach, stemming from the preeminence of the income statement and the matching concept, necessarily relies on ad hoc decisions rather than on accounting theory—on independent value judgments rather than on consistent analysis.

The Static Funds Statement View

A second approach to the balance sheet has emerged in recent years in which it is viewed primarily as a kind of static funds statement. A

14. "Accounting for the 'Investment Credit,'" APB Opinion 2 (New York: AICPA, Dec. 1962), par. 13, p. 7.

15. APB Opinion 2, par. 14, p. 7.

number of accounting textbooks describe the balance sheet in this way.[16] This development seems to have paralleled the increased attention given to reporting a summary of the transactions resulting in changes in working capital during periods of time—that is, to so-called statements of sources and applications of funds.

Raymond P. Marple has suggested in an article in *The Journal of Accountancy* that, to describe the balance sheet "as a statement of financial position, tells little about the balance sheet. It would be much more appropriate to refer to it as 'a statement of the sources and composition of company capital.' " According to Marple, "If this were done, and the form of the statement revised to better display the sources from which the capital was obtained and the forms in which it is held, the function of the balance sheet would be much clearer."[17]

In *An Inquiry Into the Nature of Accounting* Louis Goldberg contrasts the nature of the balance sheet according to the "commander" theory with the balance sheets of other theories. "If we allow ourselves to become imbued with the notion of ownership as the basis of accounting, the balance sheet becomes a statement of 'values' owned and owed; and the question of who owns and who owes is controversially but inconclusively raised. If, however, we adopt the position that the balance sheet is prepared by or on behalf of and from the point of view of a commander—the chief executive officer, be he the proprietor himself or the small group of partners or the president or managing director—it can be seen as a statement of the sources from which he has (or they have) derived resources and the directions in which those resources have been applied, and it is therefore more directly a statement of stewardship than of ownership."[18]

Another proponent of the static funds statement approach to the balance sheet has attempted to analyze a specific accounting issue from that point of view. In a recent article in the *Financial Executive* David F. Hawkins has argued that considerable progress could be

16. For example, Leonard E. Morrissey, *Contemporary Accounting Problems* (Englewood Cliffs, N.J.: Prentice-Hall, 1963), pp. 4, 44; Myron J. Gordon and Gordon Shillinglaw, *Accounting—A Management Approach*, 4th ed. (Homewood, Ill.: Richard D. Irwin, 1969), pp. 23, 497; Robert N. Anthony, *Management Accounting—Test and Cases*, 4th ed. (Homewood, Ill.: Richard D. Irwin, 1970), pp. 45, 325; Harold Bierman, Jr., and Allan R. Drebin, *Financial Accounting: An Introduction* (New York: Macmillan Co., 1968), p. 21.

17. Raymond P. Marple, "The Balance Sheet—Capital Sources and Composition," *The Journal of Accountancy* (Nov. 1962), p. 58.

18. Louis Goldberg, *An Inquiry Into the Nature of Accounting* (Evanston, Ill.: AAA, 1965), pp. 170–71.

made in resolving the controversy surrounding income tax allocation if:

> financial accounting is regarded as being concerned with maintaining a continuing record of a company's flow of financial resources;
> the balance sheet is viewed as presenting a two-sided look at a company's capital (the left-hand side reflecting where the company's capital is lodged, the right-hand side showing the current status of capital obtained from creditors, owners, and other sources);
> net income is seen as measuring principally the funds available for dividends and reinvestment obtained through the use of capital in the operations of the company; and
> it is agreed accounting for deferred taxes should reflect (1) the way businessmen handle tax considerations in capital investment decisions, (2) the way they incorporate the deferral in their financial planning, and (3) the nature of income taxes.[19]

Earlier, in a similar article in the *Harvard Business Review*, Hawkins had hailed APB Opinion 11, "Accounting for Income Taxes," as one which seems to "Encourage, in its implicit move toward the sources and uses of funds approach, the aim of corporate executives and CPAs to find ways to make more understandable a number of items on the balance sheet which cannot be explained satisfactorily to stockholders by the more traditional accounting concepts."[20]

He criticized the opinion, not because of the board's conclusion in favor of comprehensive allocation—he supports that conclusion—but because the deferred tax account is not adequately rationalized. His analysis: "In the past the deferred tax issue has revolved around the question of whether the deferral should be treated as a liability, in the traditional accounting sense. But if the right-hand side of the balance sheet is regarded as presenting the current status of a company's source of funds obtained externally, then this argument becomes irrelevant. The question should be: Is the deferral a significant enough source of funds to be disclosed on the right-hand side of the balance sheet? By its support of comprehensive allocation, the Board has indicated that

19. David F. Hawkins, "Deferred Taxes: Source of Non-Operating Funds," *Financial Executive* (Feb. 1969), p. 35.
20. David F. Hawkins, "Controversial Accounting Changes," *Harvard Business Review* (Mar.–Apr. 1968), p. 20.

this is a meaningful source of capital and that it is misleading to include it in earnings."[21]

Of course, the amount of income taxes in question inevitably shows up on the right-hand side of the balance sheet either as deferred income taxes or as retained earnings.[22] But, using a "standard of meaningful and fair disclosure of invested capital," Hawkins argues that "the capital *retained* in the business through *postponement* of income tax payments" should be separately identified as a "source of invested capital."[23] His argument, however, is self-contradictory. Capital *retained* in the business through postponement of income tax payments must necessarily have had some other source; otherwise, the capital would not have been there to be retained.

The *nonuse* of funds is not the same thing as a *source* of funds. If sources were viewed as all those things for which funds were not used, rejected capital expenditure proposals and rejected union demands would qualify. Indeed, the possibilities boggle the mind. Furthermore, it seems unlikely that Hawkins' standard of meaningful and fair disclosure of invested capital has sufficient rigor to determine which transactions can be reflected in retained earnings and which require separate identification as a source of invested capital. For example, he states that the funds approach can be extended to include "profits on sale-and-leaseback arrangements."[24] Then, how about the gain on an outright sale? And, is it only the gain that is a source of funds, or is it the entire proceeds?

The observation has been made that, although the initial balance sheet of a newly formed concern may be a good statement of funds, "at some relatively early point along the way after operations have begun, the balance sheet, standing alone, begins to lose its function as a funds statement."[25]

Although for some purposes it may be useful to equate "funds" with assets, it is unfortunate that a term so commonly used as a synonym for cash and net working capital should be given this much broader meaning as well. And, even if funds and assets may properly be used syn-

21. "Controversial Accounting Changes," p. 30.

22. This observation was also made by Lawrence Revsine in "Some Controversy Concerning 'Controversial Accounting Changes,'" *The Accounting Review* (Apr. 1969), pp. 354–58, where he examines Hawkins' analysis of accounting for income taxes in some detail.

23. "Controversial Accounting Changes," p. 32.

24. "Controversial Accounting Changes," p. 30.

25. Maurice Moonitz, "Reporting on the Flow of Funds," *The Accounting Review* (July 1956), p. 376.

onymously, any attempt to describe the nature of liabilities as sources is at best diversionary and at worst fallacious.

Balance sheets do not report the sources of the assets on hand, except perhaps coincidentally, and describing balance sheets as though they do is likely to be misleading. Frequently, liabilities arise as a result of transactions that are not even remotely related to sources of funds. For example, none of the accrued liabilities such as accrued wages, accrued interest, and accrued taxes can properly be characterized as sources of funds. The declaration of cash dividends is properly reported in a statement of sources and applications of working capital as an application; the declaration of cash dividends is not a source of funds simply because it creates a liability. If a source of additional assets is being sought, the declaration of dividends with a concomitant increase in the amount of dividends payable is not likely to be fruitful. And one can be sure that liabilities resulting from legal actions, such as the antitrust actions against certain electrical equipment manufacturers a few years ago, are not viewed by the defendants as sources of funds.

Finally, the question of relevance must be raised. Even if it were possible to prepare a balance sheet reporting at a given point of time the funds on hand and where those funds came from, for what purpose might such information be used? The potential uses of measures of "flows of funds"—sources and uses of funds during periods of time—are widely proclaimed. For example, the board of directors of the Financial Analysts Federation has endorsed the publication of statements of sources and applications of funds in corporate reports to shareholders, stating that "the analysis of a company's past and projected flow of funds can provide valuable insight into such matters as: (1) future dividend policy, (2) the financing of capital expenditures and the extent to which additional debt / or equities may be issued to finance same, and (3) the ability to meet debt service requirements. . . ."[26] Note the concern with flow of funds. Those purposes could not be fulfilled by measurements of the sources of the particular assets on hand at any given time. The relevance of the balance sheet as a static funds statement is not at all clear.

The Financial Position View

Viewed as a statement of financial position, the balance sheet represents the embodiment of the most fundamental elements of accounting

26. "News Report," *The Journal of Accountancy* (June 1964), pp. 9–10.

theory and, at the same time, provides useful information in its own right. But the structure begins with the notion of an entity.

The concept of an entity is among the most primitive elements of accounting theory. In accounting, the entity may be defined as "an area of economic interest to a particular individual or group."[27] Neither a statement of income nor a statement of financial position is feasible without first circumscribing the entity for which an accounting is to be made.

At the first level of derivation are the concepts of assets (expected future economic benefits, rights to which have been acquired by the entity as a result of some past transaction) and liabilities (the entity's obligations to convey assets or perform services, obligations resulting from past transactions and requiring settlement in the future). Once the entity is identified, one can contemplate accounting for its assets and its liabilities.

At the next level of derivation are the concepts of owners' equity or net assets (the residual interest in the assets of the entity) and income (the amount of any change in net assets during a period of time, assuming no additional investments or distributions to owners).[28] Of course, a variety of potential bases for measuring these concepts exist: invested cost in terms of numbers of dollars, invested cost in terms of purchasing power, current cost of replacing equivalent service potential, current cost of replacement in kind, current cash equivalent, etc. But, whatever the basis, it must be acknowledged that the measurement of income is dependent upon the measurement of net assets, which, in turn, is directly dependent upon the measurement of assets and liabilities.

According to this view, all transactions are analyzed in terms of their effect on assets, liabilities, and owners' equity. The measurement of income does not even require revenue and expense accounts; such accounts merely provide subsidiary information about changes in owners' equity in the same way that customers' accounts provide subsidiary information about the total amount of accounts receivable.

27. An entity is fundamental to the sheet of balances and the static funds statement, as well. For a discussion of the fundamental nature of the entity concept and the development of this definition, see 1964 Concepts and Standards Research Study Committee—The Business Entity Concept, "The Entity Concept," *The Accounting Review* (Apr. 1965), pp. 358–67.

28. These concepts of assets, liabilities, owners' equity, and income are adapted from Robert T. Sprouse and Maurice Moonitz, *A Tentative Set of Broad Accounting Principles for Business Enterprises*, ARS 3 (New York: AICPA, 1962).

This does not detract from the informational content of revenue and expense accounts. The information such accounts supply about the nature and extent of various operating transactions that give rise to changes in assets and liabilities and hence owners' equity can be extremely useful in making predictions about the results of the entity's future operations.

The financial position view does not eliminate all the problems and resolve all the controversies surrounding the analysis of accounting issues, but it does sharply limit the number of eligible alternatives and, most important, it focuses the resolution of accounting issues on fundamental concepts. As a result, it permits attention to be devoted to the refinement of those fundamental concepts rather than to the invention of new rationalizations for individual preferences.

As a statement of financial position that summarizes the assets, liabilities, and residual equity of the entity, the balance sheet is also an economic document providing useful information in its own right. The financial position of a business enterprise is the relationship of the resources available to the enterprise and the obligations of the enterprise that require the future utilization of resources. The resources reported in statements of financial position are necessarily limited to those assets that have been acquired as a result of past transactions, but the essence of reported assets is their ability to provide future economic benefits. Similarly, the liabilities reported in statements of financial position are necessarily limited to obligations that have been incurred as a result of past transactions, but the significance of reported liabilities lies in the future utilization of resources that their settlement will require.

Presumably, the financial statements supplied to current and prospective stockholders and creditors are intended to provide information about two matters of critical importance: profitability and risk. Traditionally, the income statement has been the major source of information about the former and the balance sheet the primary source of information about the latter. These two statements, however, are inextricably related. Profitability cannot really be evaluated without reference to the resources employed in creating profits, and risk cannot really be evaluated without reference to the expected results of the firm's operations. Two firms with identical income streams are not necessarily equally profitable; two firms with identical financial positions do not necessarily involve equal risk.

Balance-sheet classifications—especially the current versus noncurrent classification—and the use of financial ratios in the analysis of financial statements frequently manifest concern with financial position.[29] For example, the current ratio is a measure of the relationship of the liquid resources available to an enterprise and its most pressing future obligations—obligations that will require the use of liquid resources. We are all aware of the widespread significance attached to the current ratio, the acid test ratio, the debt / equity ratio, the average cost of capital, and other ratios, each of which depends upon meaningful content and classification in the accounts reported in the balance sheet.[30]

The task of the analyst in evaluating financial position is bound to be complicated by the sheet of balances approach, where the balance sheet serves as a dumping ground for balances that someone has decided should not be included in the income statement. The analyst's necessary reclassification of such items in attempting to determine a firm's assets and liabilities is almost certain to be based on less information than was available to the accountant.

Summary and Conclusions

In summary, let me attempt to delineate the three alternative views of the balance sheet in terms of their consequences.

The sheet of balances view of the balance sheet is an outgrowth of the notion that, by employing the matching concept, the income statement can be made superior to the balance sheet—superior in content and superior as a basis for accounting analyses. The ultimate result of a continuing extension of this view is highly predictable; a precedent exists—the *Internal Revenue Code* and the *Regulations* which interpret

29. Roy A. Foulke, vice-president of Dun and Bradstreet and author of a well-known book on financial statement analysis, advocates the use of a set of fourteen financial ratios. The numerators or denominators for thirteen of the fourteen are taken from the balance sheet; for half of the fourteen ratios, both the numerators and denominators are taken from the balance sheet. *Practical Financial Statement Analysis* (New York: McGraw-Hill Book Co., 1961).

30. In an empirical study, William H. Beaver tested the efficacy of thirty popular ratios in predicting the inability of a firm to pay its financial obligations as they mature. Of these, the best predictor—the cash-flow to total-debt ratio—proved to have excellent discriminatory power. Either the numerator or denominator was taken from the balance sheet for each of the top six predictors; for three of those six, both the numerators and denominators were taken from the balance sheet. "Financial Ratios as Predictors of Failure," *Empirical Research in Accounting: Selected Studies 1966* (Chicago: Institute of Professional Accounting, Graduate School of Business, University of Chicago, 1967), pp. 71–111.

the code. The similarities are most striking. Because no concept of taxable income exists and individuals obviously have very different opinions about appropriate components and measurements, detailed rules for its computation must be promulgated. Amendments and revocations are commonplace, as judgments about the propriety of inclusions, exclusions, and measurements change. The role of the practitioner increasingly becomes one of checking the code to determine whether clients' treatments of transactions are acceptable according to the letter of the law.

This approach to financial reporting will work. Indeed, it may be the only feasible practical solution. But the costs are extraordinarily high—costs in terms of the time and talent that must be devoted to the promulgation of detailed rules and procedures and costs in terms of the sacrifice of intellectual stimulation and personal gratification that one normally associates with the professions.

The static funds statement view leads to a drastic departure from the balance sheet as we know it. This, in itself, is not necessarily fatal, but much work needs to be done in analyzing and explaining the consequences of such a departure. For example, in what way would the income statement be related to the balance sheet if this view were fully implemented? How shall guidelines be established to distinguish between transactions that may properly be reflected in funds from operations and transactions that should be separately identified in the balance sheet as a source of invested capital? And probably most important, who is interested in a static funds statement and for what purpose?

If there is to be a theory of accounting, among these three views the financial position view of the balance sheet provides the only hope. The theory calls for the identification of an entity and an accounting for the resources and obligations of that entity. The entity's income during any period of time is based on the changes in its resources and obligations during that period, and the basic distinction is between those transactions taking place between the entity and its owners and all other transactions. Obviously, this is oversimplified; the mere adoption of a particular view of the balance sheet will not solve all the probiems of measuring financial position and income. It is, however, a necessary first step.

A few years ago one of the leading practitioners in the United States expressed his opinion that there is "a much bigger gap between the academic researchers and the practicing members of the accounting profession than in any other profession . . . including law, medicine and engineering."[31]

This gap has most likely widened still further since that statement was made. The academic emphasis is necessarily on theory, analysis, and logic—not on the memorization and unquestioning acceptance of rules that have been promulgated. The objective is to develop systematic, orderly thought processes that one can rely upon in striving to arrive at sound decisions about accounting issues as they arise and to insure that the solutions to such problems are consistent with the whole body of accounting thought. In other words, the objective of the academician is the development and application of accounting theory. To the extent that the primary intellectual ingredient in accounting is merely the experienced personal judgment of its senior practitioners, if there is no body of concepts and theories that can be utilized in the analysis of accounting problems, the study of accounting in the universities is rightfully in jeopardy.

31. Herman W. Bevis, "Progress and Poverty in Accounting Thought," *The Journal of Accountancy* (July 1966), p. 39.

Discussion of "The Balance Sheet—Embodiment of the Most Fundamental Elements of Accounting Theory"

Alfred Rappaport

WHENEVER Bob Sprouse, one of our most respected and articulate spokesmen, comments on the current scene in accounting, there is great interest in his observations. When I learned that Bob would be discussing the balance sheet, a statement relegated to obscurity by recent generations of accounting theorists, I awaited his manuscript with more than ordinary interest. I speculated at the time that, in the noblest tradition of good sportsmanship, Bob had decided to champion the cause of an underdog. The accuracy of this speculation was quickly confirmed when I read his manuscript. As a result, I find myself in the doubly unenviable position of being cast as a critic of Bob Sprouse defending an accounting underdog.

Sprouse's paper aims at providing support for the proposition that "the balance sheet embodies the most fundamental elements of accounting theory from which the essential elements contained in the income statement are necessarily derived." In support of this proposition, three views of the balance sheet (the sheet of balances view, the static funds statement view, and the financial position view) are examined. From this analysis, Sprouse concludes that one view, the financial position view, is superior to the other two. My purpose here is to examine briefly the claimed primacy for the balance sheet in accounting theory development and Sprouse's assessment of various balance-sheet approaches or views. In addition, I propose to offer for your consideration a fourth balance-sheet view.

Consider, first, Sprouse's initial proposition. It is important to recognize that this proposition is based on a structural or designer's view of the accounting system, not on the user's or consumer's view. Sprouse appropriately makes this distinction at the very beginning of his paper by accepting the primacy of the income statement in terms of user interest; on the structural or logical form level, he suggests that "concepts of assets and liabilities are more fundamental than the concept of income" since the latter depends upon the former. The relative merits of the structural-versus-user view of the accounting system will be discussed subsequently. First, let us turn our attention to Sprouse's structurally based argument on the primacy of the balance sheet.

The structural view offers no explicit user decision models or behavioral theory to provide guidelines for choice among alternative configurations of information. Instead, such a view in accounting is characterized by the implicit assumption that the duality framework per se, including the necessary articulation between the balance sheet and income statements, is in some general sense useful and hence should be accepted a priori. Sprouse, using a structurally based argument, contends that the balance sheet embodies more fundamental elements of accounting theory than the income statement. The purported rationale for this contention would presumably include the following statements: (a) "the income statement can properly be described as merely a summary of one class of transactions resulting in changes in one balance sheet account"; (b) "the measurement of income is dependent upon the measurement of net assets which, in turn, is dependent upon the measurement of assets and liabilities"; and (c) "no one has ever successfully managed to formulate a concept of income that is not directly or indirectly dependent upon the concept of assets and the concept of liabilities."

For purposes of direct contrast, consider the following three alternative propositions:

a) The balance sheet can properly be described as a summary of stocks or residuals that results from income statement transactions.

b) The measurement of net assets is dependent upon the measurement of income, which, in turn, is dependent upon the measurement of revenue and expenses.

c) No one has ever successfully managed to formulate a concept of assets that is not directly or indirectly dependent upon a concept of income.

Is this set of three propositions more accurate than the Sprouse set enumerated earlier? Or is the Sprouse set perhaps more accurate? Adhering once again to the structural or logical form approach to accounting systems, we are necessarily indifferent about these two sets of propositions. Within the context of an explicitly defined analytical system such as the accounting double-entry system, one can define a given systems variable in terms of other systems variables. For example, a system with only two variables, a and i, can be described in terms of $a = f(i)$ or $i = f(a)$. If we were to adopt a somewhat oversimplified view of the accounting system, we would perhaps designate i to represent income and a, net assets. The two propositions $a = f(i)$ and $i = f(a)$ are analytic rather than synthetic propositions, since their validity depends solely on the definitions of the symbols they contain rather than on empirical observation.[1]

Returning for a moment to Sprouse's set of three propositions, note that the first two propositions are essentially two ways of asserting $i = f(a)$, while the third proposition is simply a logical consequence of the first two. As you would expect, the first two of my three alternative propositions assert that $a = f(i)$, and the third proposition is once again a logical consequence of the first two.

The important point to emphasize here is that the structural approach to accounting systems does not admit exogenously derived postulated systems objectives, and hence there is no logical basis for choosing one systems representation over another. For our specific purposes, the structural approach allows us no basis for choice between the Sprouse propositions and the alternative propositions. Fortunately, we are not at an impasse, since Sprouse implicitly rejects the structural view as he begins his discussion of the three balance-sheet views.

Unlike the structural approach, the user approach to accounting theory is based upon some user decision model or models. While Sprouse does not explicitly present a user model, it is reasonable to assume that some underlying user model was employed to rank one approach to balance-sheet measures—the financial position view—above two alternative approaches—the sheet of balances view and the static funds statement view. In the absence of an explicit designation of user

1. Alfred Jules Ayer, *Language, Truth and Logic* (New York: Dover Publications, 1952), pp. 78–79.

models, there is no logical basis for either acknowledging or denying the validity of Sprouse's balance-sheet preferences. In light of this, I propose to offer a number of general observations about the three balance-sheet views and then briefly discuss a fourth view based on a postulated user decision model.

Let us begin with the sheet of balances approach, which views the balance sheet "as a summary of debit and credit account balances that remain after the determinants of income have been decided upon and the retained earnings account has been adjusted for the amount of income that results." Surely the contention that this approach is not likely to result in a particularly useful statement is a foregone conclusion, assuming even a relatively wide spectrum of different user models. Is the basic problem simply the treatment of the balance sheet as a secondary or residual statement, or is there perhaps a more fundamental problem? I submit that the real answer lies in the futility of implementing the matching concept. As Sprouse forcefully states, "the matching concept necessarily relies on ad hoc decisions rather than on accounting theory—on independent value judgments rather than on consistent analysis." This observation is not only central to the Sprouse paper, but in large measure helps explain the difficulty facing accountants today. In light of its significance, I would like to elaborate on the measurement problems associated with the matching concept.

If we were to develop present-value financial statements under conditions of perfect certainty, the results would be identical whether we treated the balance sheet or the income statement as the residual statement. Residual approaches such as the sheet of balances approach affect results only when means of dealing with uncertainty are required.

What has been the accountant's response to uncertainty? Conservatism, consistency, increasing disclosure, and demands for objectivity as manifested by adherence to historical cost conventions represent key mechanisms for dealing with uncertainty. Consider the serious income-determination problems found in the cost-matching area. The cost-matching decision, that is the decision concerning the assignment of costs as deductions from revenue in specific accounting periods, reflects the accountant's broad perception of the relative risks associated with cost outlays. Accountants appear to be concerned with two types of risk—economic and measurement.[2] An economic risk may be

2. The term "measurement" is used here only in the general sense of assigning numbers to real world phenomena according to rules.

viewed as the probability that an outlay will result in no net benefit to the firm. Where the economic risk is judged to be high, the outlay is treated as an expense in the same period as the commitment for the outlay is incurred. Costs associated with pure research serve as an outstanding example of a high-risk outlay generally treated as an expense.

Measurement risks are best characterized as the uncertainties of implementing the matching principle. High measurement risks occur when either it is difficult to identify the tangible benefits or revenues arising from certain costs (e.g., executive salaries paid largely for planning activities, campaigns to promote company name and products, executive and employee educational programs, administrative facilities such as buildings and information systems, philanthropic contributions) or when estimates of the magnitude and timing of benefits are subject to a significant degree of error (e.g., product improvement programs, patents, copyrights, new productive facilities). The accountant's reaction to the basic forms of measurement risk can be summarized as follows:

Measurement risk	*Measurement procedure*
1. Difficult to identify revenues arising from a given cost.	1. Expense in current period.
2. Estimated time duration of expected benefit or revenue flow subject to significant measurement error.	2. Expense in current period.
3. Estimated time duration of expected benefits subject to relatively small margins of error, but magnitude and timing of benefit or revenue flows subject to significant measurement error.	3. Choice of a systematic write-off basis over the estimated time duration of expected benefits.

It should be clearly recognized that, while the three measurement-risk categories enumerated above may broadly indicate the basis for the accountant's choice of a measurement procedure, there is ample evidence to suggest that accountants evaluating a given cost outlay may in many cases not agree upon the appropriate measurement-risk category for the outlay. The accountant's subjective assessment of management's expectations for, say, research and development outlays will influence the choice between measurement risk no. 2 (expense in current period) and measurement risk no. 3 (systematic write-off). Furthermore, the choice of measurement risk no. 3 leads to a wide range of possibilities of systematic write-off patterns. Indeed, it is useful to view the basic income-determination alternatives as constituting the intersection between management-risk categories no. 2 and no. 3 plus the discretionary measurement alternatives available within measurement-risk category no. 3. Indeed, one can reluctantly view many of the controversies in accounting today as essentially a debate between uniform arbitrariness and flexible arbitrariness.[3] In summing up the sheet of balance view, I submit that its failings derive from, in Sprouse's words, "the matching concept (which) necessarily relies on ad hoc decisions rather than on accounting theory—on independent value judgments rather than on consistent analysis."

The static funds statement view, so named because it purports to show the sources and composition of company capital at a prescribed point in time, is rejected by Sprouse on grounds that it is not feasible, and, secondly, even if it were feasible, the relevance or usefulness of such disclosure is questioned. As is the case with the sheet of balances view, the lack of feasibility of the static funds statement view is clearly attributable to the accountant's difficulty in coping with uncertainty. The question of relevance is best deferred in the absence of an explicit user model.

Of the three balance-sheet views, Sprouse clearly prefers the financial position view. Indeed, he suggests that, "if there is to be a theory of accounting, the financial position view of the balance sheet provides the only hope." The evidence to support such a far-reaching assertion is far from apparent. Indeed, it is difficult to reconcile Sprouse's forceful presentation on the futility of the matching concept with his advocacy of the financial position view which depends directly on matching.

The distinctions between the financial position view and the other views proposed are not sharply delineated. For example, the description of the financial position view as "the relationship of the resources available to the enterprise and the obligations of the enterprise that require the future utilization of resources" is uncomfortably close to the static funds statement view of the balance sheet as "a statement of the sources and composition of company capital." Nor is it clear whether

3. For a comprehensive demonstration of the arbitrariness of accounting allocations, see Arthur L. Thomas, *The Allocation Problem in Financial Accounting Theory* (Evanston, Ill.: AAA, 1969).

the financial position and the sheet of balances views are antithetical.

Sprouse suggests that stockholders and investors should be provided information about a firm's earning power and solvency. If we impose the constraints of current practice, that balance sheets and income statements must articulate with one another and that historical cost be employed, then it is quite possible to find important situations in which the goals of providing information about earning power and solvency may be in conflict. Consider, for example, the question of alternative inventory cost methods. Because LIFO, in most circumstances, generates a better matching of current costs with current revenues, it may result in a better indication of a firm's earning power than other methods such as FIFO or average cost. In a growing firm and under inflationary conditions, LIFO inventory cost appearing on the balance sheet may, however, be significantly less than current cost. The adoption of FIFO is likely to lead to the reverse situation. The advocate of the sheet of balances view would presumably choose the LIFO method since he is more willing to tolerate shortcomings in the balance sheet than in the income statement. Would the financial position advocate suggest FIFO under these conditions? Perhaps he would, but Sprouse has not set forth how he would logically assess information trade-offs between the balance sheet and the income statement.

One final observation concerning the financial position view warrants comment. Sprouse's preference for the financial position view appears to be based largely on the usefulness of balance-sheet outputs for assessing probable failure or insolvency. While this focus is particularly useful for creditors in extremely risky firms, there should be equal concern for the informational needs of investors in the vast majority of going concerns. Whether this broader notion of the accountant's audience would change Sprouse's preference ordering is once again dependent upon postulated user models.

At this point I would like to note a fourth possible view of the balance sheet recently presented by the AAA 1966–1968 Committee on External Reporting. In its attempt to develop information useful to equity investors and creditors, the committee outlined the following steps:

1. Select normative investors' and creditors' valuation models. The committee selected a dividend model for equity investors.

2. Select a model for the prediction of dividends and other distributions to stockholders and creditors.

3. List object and activity inputs (potentially relevant identifications of items and events) and their related attributes and measurement concepts.

4. Evaluate each of the attributes of each object or activity input for relevancy (its ability to permit a prediction of a variable or relationship in the models).

5. List potentially acceptable measurement procedures.

6. Assess each procedure for each attribute in light of the standards of quantifiability, verifiability, and freedom from bias.

7. Select the attributes and measurement procedures that should be included in financial reports.[4]

Using the foregoing approach, some of the committee's broad recommendations are as follows:

1. External financial reports should include at least a statement of resources and commitments and a statement showing current monetary flows such as those suggested in exhibits A and B. These two statements should complement one another in analyses for forecasting future cash flows. The statement of resources should include information regarding objects likely to contribute to future cash flows and the report of commitments should represent probable future outflows. The current monetary flow statement should represent an enumeration of changes in resources and commitments.

2. External financial reports should be expected to "balance" or articulate with each other. In fact, we find that forced balancing and articulation have frequently restricted the presentation of relevant information.

3. Reported information should not be restricted to that which can be expressed in dollar terms. Wherever they meet the standards adequately, physical measures, classifications, and nonquantifiable descriptions should be included in reports in addition to monetary measurements.[5]

Perhaps at this juncture the committee's methodology is more interesting and useful than its recommendations. In my view, however, employing the user's approach to accounting theory, not the struc-

4. "An Evaluation of External Reporting Practices: A Report of the 1966–68 Committee on External Reporting," *The Accounting Review*, Supplement to vol. 44 (1969), p. 80.

5. "An Evaluation of External Reporting Practices," pp. 117–18.

tural or designer's approach, holds the greatest hope for progress in accounting theory. The structural approach to accounting theory, which treats balance-sheet income statement articulation as axiomatic, seriously limits the search for more useful information constructs. The fourth view of the balance sheet presented as exhibit A, which some may wish to refer to as the nonbalancing balance-sheet view, must, as any other proposed disclosure, meet certain empirical standards of usefulness. On the other hand, it should be noted that this, as well as other innovative departures from current practice, can be logically derived from the user's approach, but not the structural approach to accounting theory. Therefore, I submit that the question of whether or not the balance sheet as we know it today embodies the most fundamental elements of accounting theory is not as crucial as the question of what recommendations would result from vigorously developed accounting theory based on user needs. It is at least open to debate whether any of the conventional balance-sheet views would survive such inquiry.

In closing, let me emphasize that while Bob Sprouse and I may have some differences over research methodology, I am in absolute agreement with his fundamental observation that "if there is no body of concepts and theories that can be utilized in the analysis of accounting problems, the study of accounting in the universities is rightfully in jeopardy."

What is the Message of "A Statement of Basic Accounting Theory"?

Harvey T. Deinzer

HAVING MADE an early study of the report by an AAA committee entitled ASOBAT (*A Statement of Basic Accounting Theory*), I urgently requested more of the good things which a document of that sort should have—support and development, explicitness, and rigorous precision.

Contributions to the support and development of the ASOBAT message may be identifiable in the more than fifty articles citing ASOBAT which have been published in major accounting journals in the United States since the auspicious birth of that document in 1966. My experiences in reviewing the ASOBAT gloss have been that the interpretations of the ASOBAT theory structure and of the meanings for the committee's practice recommendations have been diverse. The degree of diversity on those matters is sufficient to motivate renewed research into the structure and functioning of the technique presented for connecting practices with the represented theory. Indefiniteness in ASOBAT specifications of theory and practices suggests that the ASOBAT description of bridging operations has also elicited varying interpretations. The major question in this paper relates to the grounds on which the ASOBAT assertions rest, and the conclusion is reached that the ASOBAT expressions on roles for standards are not unified.

One proposition that can be considered established is that the ASOBAT committee emphasizes a practical role for standards, as the task of selecting / rejecting accounting methods. The ASOBAT message is more than an admonition to think relevantly, more than a prompting to raise the question of what is relevant. Otherwise, the association's Executive Committee would not have assigned a short-term responsibility, subsequently, to the AAA Committee on External Reporting, for indicating the modifications in contemporary practices required by an application of the ASOBAT standards.

For the methods selection task, it was of prime importance to the committee that criteria be solidly placed on foundation concepts. Only on a concepts foundation would the standards serve as yardsticks.

Interpretation of the ASOBAT Standards is Unsettled

Interpretation of the ASOBAT standards is unsettled with respect both to subjects for discrimination and to processes of treatment. The intended subjects for discrimination by application of the standards may have been broader in scope than accounting methods.

TYPES OF ENTITIES DISCRIMINATED

In that combination of ASOBAT document and commentary literature which may be called "the annotated ASOBAT," the standards could be applied to various entities. Among these are accounting methods, procedures, practices;[1] consequences, potentials of accounting methods;[2] items, data, information, or potential accounting information.[3] Subjects for discrimination could include attributes of economic data, such attributes together with their implicated measurement rules, the measurement procedures (at least initially), or values produced by measurement procedures implicated in the identified attributes.[4] The scope of attributes could range from the particular attribute of predictiveness for future cash flows[5] to attributes whose values may exist

1. ASOBAT (Evanston, Ill.: AAA, 1966), pp. 1, 6.

2. ASOBAT, p. 8.

3. ASOBAT, pp. 3, 7, 8. Billy E. Goetz, "Transfer Prices: An Exercise in Relevancy and Goal Congruence," *The Accounting Review* (July 1967), p. 435. Keith Shwayder, "Relevance," *Journal of Accounting Research* (Spring 1968), p. 86. Howard J. Snavely, "Accounting Information Criteria," *The Accounting Review* (Apr. 1967), p. 223.

4. AAA, Committee on External Reporting, "An Evaluation of External Reporting Practices," *Supplement to The Accounting Review* (Evanston, Ill., 1969), pp. 88–89.

5. Committee on External Reporting, p. 118.

by definition only.[6] The relationship of standards to theory structures might be such that their employment could discriminate among accounting models[7] or decision models.[8] Even matters of accounting propriety[9] could come under the operation of the standards. Or the standards could be used to discriminate among the standards themselves, in respect to measurability.[10]

COMPLETENESS OF THE STANDARDS SET

The standards are structurally represented by the ASOBAT committee as essential parts of a foundation of concepts.[11] Their function is that of a comparison tool (yardstick or benchmark), with respect to dealings with, at least, the operational processes of accountants in financial reporting. Is the set of selection criteria presented in ASOBAT too limited in its breadth of applicability or in its sensitivity?

The association's Committee on External Reporting, which was charged with evaluating current accounting practices under the illumination afforded by the ASOBAT standards, would have added a fifth standard, that of probable social and economic effects.[12] Another group probing the functioning of the ASOBAT standards, the association's Committee on Managerial Decision Models, emphasized the problem of exercising choice among alternative modes of conduct of particular importance in the area of internal reporting. That committee suggested the addition of a fifth standard called an economic feasibility criterion,[13] although the net effect might be four standards if the quantifiability standard were to be eliminated. Another criterion deemed neglected by the ASOBAT committee under ASOBAT annotations was understandability.

THE STANDARDS AS PROPERTIES OF ACCOUNTING INFORMATION

Absence of an ASOBAT specification of observable traits subject to evaluatory judgment, in combination with committee expression of feelings about degrees in which the relevance standard is contained in one or another accounting treatment pattern, may have been the basis

6. Committee on External Reporting, p. 89.

7. Joel S. Demski, "Predictive Ability of Alternative Performance Measurement Models," *Journal of Accounting Research* (Spring 1969), p. 97.

8. AAA, Committee on Managerial Decision Models, "Report," *Supplement to The Accounting Review* (Evanston, Ill., 1969), p. 43.

9. ASOBAT, p. 2.

10. ASOBAT, p. 3.

11. ASOBAT, p. 3.

12. Committee on External Reporting, p. 95.

13. Committee on Managerial Decision Models, p. 52.

for a judgment that the ASOBAT set implicitly includes adequacy as a fifth standard.[14] If the standards do operate to identify properties or characteristics of accounting information to which the standards' names are attached, such properties are variously named, and some lack of collation with the ASOBAT titles and apparent distinctions is evident in the commentary literature.

Relevance.—In one interpretation in which the standards are definitions of properties of accounting information, the ASOBAT standard of relevance is replaced by objectivity. In several instances, objectivity is closely associated with some combination of verifiability and freedom from bias. In another interpretation, the term that replaces "relevance" is "realization," while another commentator regards the realization criterion as instrumental in fixing a *time* of relevancy.

Freedom-from-Bias.—Interpretation of the standard of freedom-from-bias was troublesome, since, as stated by the Committee on Managerial Decision Models, "bias is never explicitly defined in the Statement."[15] In its reading of the ASOBAT document, the 1966 committee adopted the notion that "there is some universal true value with which any accounting measurement can be associated."[16] Deviations from the true value are ascribable either to perceptive weaknesses randomly distributed among personal observers or to inappropriateness of choice of modes of dealing with the materials under observation. The resulting biases are denominated personal or statistical; the latter is also termed a bias of the measurement system.

Measurement-system bias is thought to be closely associated with the standard of relevance, while personal bias is interpreted as an aspect of the standard of verifiability. However, measurement-system bias is also brought within the ambit of the standard of verifiability, in association with the standard of relevance, through inquiry into the problem of attaining the most accurate description of a property or an attribute. Application of the standard of relevance is thought to be wholly or highly conceptual, and this standard is characterized as the essential or indispensable standard. Application of the standard of freedom-from-statistical-bias, however, is deemed to require existential or operational specification.[17] A crucial question, raised by the

14. Ernest L. Hicks, "Comments on 'A Statement of Basic Accounting Theory,'" *The Journal of Accountancy* (Sept. 1966), p. 58.
15. Committee on Managerial Decision Models, p. 49.
16. Committee on Managerial Decision Models, p. 50.
17. Committee on Managerial Decision Models, p. 50.

Committee on External Reporting, is whether the degree of approximation to "the most accurate description" is measurable.[18]

Verifiability.—While the notion of verifiability is interpreted to encompass both types of freedom-from-bias, its meaning is even more extensive. Verifiability is seen as an aspect of reliability,[19] and the function of the verifiability standard is "protecting the user from arbitrary subjective judgments" by the developers of the data[20] and maintaining the confidence of the user in accounting reports.[21] Confidence of the users might be enhanced through a policy of documentation which discloses the assumptions and processing for the reported data.[22] Users could then better estimate the measurement-system bias.

Quantifiability and Measurability.—There is some question whether the ASOBAT standard of quantifiability should either be rejected as a standard or merged with a replacement standard of measurability. The Committee on Managerial Decision Models thought it possible, and even likely, that "quantifiability was designated as a standard to justify a broad view of what is to be called accounting information." The ASOBAT stress on a quantifiability standard might contribute to an undesirable submergence of some relevant information even where nonquantified information is admitted through the reporting gates.[23]

The Committee on External Reporting interpreted ASOBAT as comprehending quantification within the meaning of measurement, without elaborating the functional role of quantification in measurement operations. Instead, conclusions about quantifiability were thought, in that committee's interpretation of ASOBAT, to determine reportability as a policy matter. Little recognition is evident in the commentary literature of the "instrumental reference of quantified propositions to an intended objective consequence."[24]

THE APPLICATIONS PROCESS

Ambiguities and difficulties in an applications process for the ASOBAT standards are documented in the reports of the two AAA committees

18. Committee on External Reporting, p. 95.
19. Snavely, p. 228.
20. Committee on External Reporting, p. 48.
21. ASOBAT, p. 27. W. W. Cooper, N. Dopuch, and T. F. Keller, "Budgetary Disclosure and Other Suggestions for Improving Accounting Reports," *The Accounting Review* (Oct. 1968), p. 643.
22. Committee on Managerial Decision Models, p. 48.
23. Committee on Managerial Decision Models, p. 52.
24. John Dewey, *Logic: The Theory of Inquiry* (New York: Holt, Rinehart and Winston, 1938), p. 206.

referred to earlier in this paper. The Committee on External Reporting thought that it had identified a logical process of application, with the effect that the standards had become partly, but not fully, operational. And that committee laid down some pointers in the direction of full operationality. Other writers also offered their recommendations for moving from the ASOBAT expressions to operational or more operational standards. The external reporting committee's logical process involves an initial application of the relevance standard for the identification of relevant attributes. The other standards are introduced into the process only subsequently, for discriminating among the measurement rules implicated in the identified attributes. Only in a special case would subsequent reference to the standard of relevance be required.

In all of the proposals for applying a standard of relevance as an initial sequential step in an applications process, there is a question whether ASOBAT has been correctly interpreted. For the ASOBAT committee said that it "believes that the process of judging accounting information should involve a combined and simultaneous consideration of all four standards"[25] and that candidates for the status of accounting information are to be judged in reference to the "criteria, taken *as* a whole,"[26] not *on* the whole.

Interpretation of the Standards: An Unraveling Process

The preceding materials have been presented to evidence a lack of clarity in the ASOBAT message. In view of the importance attaching to expressions on accounting standards by committees of the AAA, serious effort should be directed to providing ordered interpretations of such recommendations. The possibility that the ASOBAT standards do not have a unified meaning is suggested by the varied interpretations of commentators on the subjects for discriminatory treatment—completeness of the standards set and relations among the proposed standards. Additional issues relate to a process of operationalizing the standards.

It may be the case that an unraveling process is required, in which mixed strands of meanings for the ASOBAT standards will become apparent. Resolution of questions of meanings for the standards does not, however, control issues of suitability of the ASOBAT expression for the resolution of those problems which stimulated the ASOBAT activity.

The remainder of this paper is concerned with the annotated expres-

25. ASOBAT, pp. 9–10.
26. ASOBAT, p. 8 (italics added).

sion of structural and functional relations between the standards and suggested theories, and with the yardstick quality which the ASOBAT committee attributed to the standards expressions. The analysis first follows the obvious lead of the committee, that the standards are concepts which are parts of some more comprehensive system of ideas. The analysis next follows another ASOBAT lead to the firing line of deciding-acting, where discriminations are made by individuals as part of a biologic process of fulfilling needs. Among the discriminations possible at this level are selections among data, including modes of symbolic presentation developed by accounting sources.

Any attempted analysis of the ASOBAT standards must take account of the representation that the standards are advocated by the ASOBAT committee for use by professional accountants, as aids in a process of both selecting and ordering symbols for presentation to decision-makers.

THE STANDARDS AS UNIVERSALS

The ASOBAT committee indicated that the standards are to become known by examining their essential nature,[27] which suggests a notion embedded in Platonian philosophy. Only reluctantly would one attribute to the ASOBAT committee acceptance of a Platonian view of knowledge. In that system, knowing proceeds by apprehension of the essential ideas, which are realities manifested in the changing phenomena observable through sensory organs. My reluctance to interpret portions of ASOBAT in Platonian terms prevails even after noting the ASOBAT committee's appeal to "a sense of reason and good judgment" as arbiter of issues on the containment of the standards in probed environmental situations.[28]

Another direction of examination of the essential nature of the standards is toward structural relationships of those standards as concepts within a larger set of ideas. The commentary literature has noted an approach to identification of theoretical reference frames for the ASOBAT standards by way of definitions of the term "accounting." Among the candidates for the ASOBAT committee's frame of ideas are an economizing theory, a measurement-communication theory, and even a developing management theory. The ASOBAT presentation ostensibly emphasizes the division of an all-inclusive criterion of usefulness

27. ASOBAT, p. 8. Cf. Peter A. Firmin and James J. Linn, "Information Systems and Managerial Accounting," *The Accounting Review* (Jan. 1968), p. 77.
28. ASOBAT, p. 18.

into four standards. The suggested Aristotelian interpretation of the standards as demarcated ontological substances is here rejected, in deference to a position that modern accounting scholars have been emancipated from Aristotelian doctrines. Instead, the more favorable interpretation is presented—that the ASOBAT definitions of accounting are doors into rooms of ideas and that the standards are elliptic references to components of the suggested theory set.

Issue of the ASOBAT-Referenced Theory.—An early reviewer of the ASOBAT document thought he knew what the referenced theory was, and he saw the standards (or most of them) as following readily from a measurement-communication theory. The most emphatic ASOBAT reference to an information theory which involved accounting as a measurement operation is in the chapter on accounting of the future. And it was that source for citation which is favored by those writers who select the information-measurement reference-frame for characterizing the ASOBAT theory.

There is some question whether the material in the future-oriented chapter 5 should be taken as a characterization of the view of the majority committee on the ASOBAT document. That chapter can be regarded as a specially formed appendix to the main document. According to the chairman of the ASOBAT committee, chapter 5 was created to receive ideas and recommendations which in the committee's view could not be implemented in the near future.[29] Elsewhere the ASOBAT document refers to measurement and presents the notion of communication guidelines as complementary to information development.

Even where the ASOBAT committee associated development of accounting information with its communication, it explains the role of accounting savants in the social process by placing them in the position of observers. The accountant is "an observer of economic or related activities . . . which he records in abstract form using descriptive words or numbers."[30] The accountant develops his picture by a process of abstraction. As observers, accountants identify information for purposes of a subsequent operation of communicating. The result of the accountant's observation and abstraction is the presentation, through reporting, of "an accurate model or picture of the underlying activity."[31] It is the "abstract expression of the activities of acquiring,

29. Charles T. Zlatkovich, "A New Accounting Theory Statement," *The Journal of Accountancy* (Aug. 1966), p. 36.
30. ASOBAT, p. 18.
31. ASOBAT, p. 18.

using, and disposing of economic resources" which relates accounting methods to an accounting methodology.[32]

There is an overlap in the criteria governing development and communication of accounting information, despite the temporal antecedence of information development. Appropriate technical activities within the accountant class, on whom the major burden of analyzing and synthesizing operations in unstructured reporting situations is placed, could ease the burden on users, of "understanding the measurement process."[33] The ASOBAT committee buttressed its commentary on a set of communication guidelines by referring to that component of an elicited communication theory which it terms the basic essentials.[34]

It has been noted that some of the commentaries on ASOBAT elect to single out the ASOBAT association of accounting with measurement-communication theory and to amplify the references to measurement theory or to communication theory, which in ASOBAT are only minimally audible. This eclectic process tends to overlook the other methodological strands in the document. More importantly, communication theory is related to accounting through mechanical analogies, utilizing the notions of sender, receiver, channel, or filter. Thus, the term "filter" is the analogue of the accountants' notion of "transaction." If the ASOBAT-referenced communication model is the engineering-statistical model of Shannon and Weaver, then appeal to it is also adjudged inappropriate, for "formal information theory has little to contribute to accounting except insofar as the *general* concepts help us to organize our thinking."[35]

To the extent that ASOBAT concentrates on a referent of engineering or statistical communication theory, the interpretation that ASOBAT newly introduces the viewpoint that "measurements in accounting are a function of some end" may be questioned.[36] The expression might better be limited to a personal statement that "accounting ought to be a measurement system"[37] and the meaning of measurement should be sought in some vital (not merely formal) context.

32. ASOBAT, p. 6.
33. ASOBAT, p. 18.
34. ABSOBAT, p. 14.
35. Robert R. Sterling, "A Statement of Basic Accounting Theory: A Review Article," *Journal of Accounting Research* (Spring 1967), p. 105.
36. Sterling, "A Statement of Basic Accounting Theory," p. 100.
37. Robert R. Sterling, "The Going Concern: An Examination," *The Accounting Review* (July 1968), p. 499.

Support of an income-maximizing interpretation for the ASOBAT theory can begin with the early definition of accounting in relation to economizing. The income-maximizing choice for the theory framework seems to account more readily for ASOBAT's heavy emphasis on usefulness qualities than does an engineering or statistical version of measurement-communication theory. This choice is supported also by a committee member's representation of dominance for a user theory viewpoint within the ASOBAT committee.[38] Writers have attempted to modify a perceived utilitarian framework in ASOBAT in the direction of providing it with operational characteristics.

Are the ASOBAT standards implicated ideas in both measurement-communication theory and micro-economic theory, as well as in a developing array of decision models of special interest for internal accounting? Would different standards follow the adoption of more behaviorally oriented theories for accounting application, where the "models . . . provide a conceptual representation of realities"?[39] Are the standards components of a single well-recognized and generally accepted theory base?[40]

Necessity and Sufficiency of Standards.—Whatever the particular theory to which the ASOBAT standards are relatable, the ASOBAT committee emphasized the qualities of the standards as necessary and sufficient to that basic accounting theory.[41] Two points should be noted: First, necessity and sufficiency are properties of meanings in respect to their relation to other meanings in a set. Goals for meanings-sets feature substitutability and equivalence. Attainment of these goals requires precision of meaning and articulation of components. For example, ambiguity in the meaning of "triangularity" would be detrimental to the necessity and sufficiency of that term for the abstract system of plane geometry. Second, the term "theory" as used in the present section, on standards as universals, follows the interpreted ASOBAT limitation of that term to idea structures.

The AAA's Executive Committee had charged the ASOBAT committee to develop a guide which had the characteristics of clarity and groundedness. Evidence for those traits would be in the explanation made and the support provided. The notion of "groundedness" needs some fur-

38. George H. Sorter, "An 'Events' Approach to Basic Accounting Theory," *The Accounting Review* (Jan. 1969), p. 12.

39. Committee on Managerial Decision Models, p. 46.

40. John T. Wheeler, "Accounting Theory and Research in Perspective," *The Accounting Review* (Jan. 1970), p. 10.

41. ASOBAT, p. 3.

ther comments because of the prevalence of a building foundations analogy in accounting thought.

In controlled inquiry (or inquiry, for short), the development of grounds for adopting particular leading principles of conduct involves the employment of theories in the narrow sense indicated previously: ideas, concepts, meanings systems, sometimes termed conceptual or ideational materials of inquiry. Sole reference to systems of meanings is not sufficient for grounding inferences among existential singulars. One cannot move from the generals of spaceless, timeless meanings to particulars of the environment. Instead, inference moves through propositions about relations among singulars, and groundedness of such inferences relates to the warranted ordering of particulars, as singulars, into *kinds* of existential objects. Since propositions about kinds of objects are also general propositions, the notion of "moving from the general to the particular" is also ambiguous.

The distinction between existential and ideational propositions is not subject to a criticism that concepts are one extreme of a continuous range, of which precepts are the other extreme. The latter, psychologically oriented distinctions are irrelevant to the identification of logical materials in terms of discriminated functions which the types of materials serve in controlled inquiry. Both types of materials are necessarily involved in the process by which propositions of two sorts acquire warranted assertibility: propositions of implications among definitional and operational elements of a meanings system and propositions of interinvolved potentialities for changes among existential objects. The intimacy of association of conceptual and existential materials in inquiry has been recognized through the term "conjugate" as expressive of that relation. Formulation of a theory consisting of meanings following as the consequences of applying specified operations to the adopted entities of the meanings-system is controlled, with respect to its suitability for existential reference, by the traits which are found to establish relations among existential materials. So much for the elaboration of the notion of groundedness.

In the interpretation of the ASOBAT standards as derivatives of sets of ideas extant in a discipline, they are necessary, essential, timeless, spaceless, and universal. In this abstract sense, they have no necessary applicability to practical affairs. In their role as universals, the implicated ideas are ideally precise and articulate in ways necessary and essential to the frame of associated meanings constituting the referenced theory. In this sense the standards as implicated ideas may be necessary and sufficient to a theory, although the ASOBAT identification of a theory and of the standards as component ideas is weak.

But in this use, trade-off is ruled out by definition and expected functioning. And a hierarchy among necessary meanings is arbitrary except in relation to a functional employment in ordering existential affairs.

Some Views on Conceptual Standards.—Concentration on an implicatory aspect of ideas is sometimes referred to as a conceptual activity. It was not clear that the commentary literature used the term "conceptual standard" in the sense of an implicatory relationship. Relevance was called a conceptual standard, and even the only conceptual standard within the ASOBAT group. The other ideas from the ASOBAT list of standards, possibly excepting quantifiability, were assertedly involved in notions of dealings with existential materials, and were placed in a feasibility or materiality class of standards or criteria.[42] Justification for the separation was expressed as a distinction between kinds and qualities of information.[43]

In some representations of relationships among ideas-in-system, the usefulness concept, with respect to which relevance is assertedly a derivative, should be placed at the apex of a hierarchy of standards, all of which are conceptual.[44] The positioning of a concept within a hierarchial structure may reflect an argument that a subordinated concept does not partake of the essence or substance of accounting.[45]

What Control Function for Universals?—Is it the status of primacy which gives to the relevance standard the quality of a necessary characteristic for all accounting information? Since the other three standards do not have this position of primacy, is the quality of being a necessary characteristic of accounting information also lacking for the latter standards?[46] If the standards are spaceless and timeless categories or abstract concepts, on what grounds is it asserted that such meanings, individually or in their relationships, exert *any* influence over existential materials of the environment? Referral of the standards to more comprehensive concept structures, denominated theories, does not remove the question of the averred functioning of the theory structure in the existential ordering of accounting practices.

42. Daniel L. McDonald, "Feasibility Criteria for Accounting Measures," *The Accounting Review* (Oct. 1967), p. 666. Shwayder, p. 87.

43. McDonald, p. 663.

44. Snavely, p. 223.

45. Snavely, p. 229, contra Goldberg.

46. ASOBAT, p. 9.

It seems clear that the 1966 committee was concerned with conditions for grounding inferences such that an experienced involvement with a question of choosing an accounting method could be resolved by taking account of certain environmental conditions. The ASOBAT committee emphasized a trade-off operation in presenting its standards. While trade-off among ideas which are ideally precise and articulate to form a meanings-system is a contradiction, trade-off among existential materials as means for reaching personal goals is an observed operation. If the standards are essential and necessary components of an articulated system of meanings, then one would not expect to find that "distinctions between . . . the standards . . . can frequently become fuzzy."[47]

Interpretation of the ASOBAT standards as universals accounts for some but not all of the expressions emphasized in the ASOBAT document. Possibly, then, ASOBAT employed at least two meanings for the term "standards." In one meaning, the standards were abstract universals. In another meaning, the standards referred to acts of existential discrimination with respect to goal attainment where the acts were taken to be reflections of tacitly known bases of comparison / contrast. In our view, ASOBAT employed the notion of standards in a third role also, in connection with their representation as guides for the class of accountants.

STANDARDS AS NAMES FOR GOAL-RELATED EXISTENTIAL DISCRIMINATIONS

At this point, attention is invited to the ASOBAT meaning of standards as placeholder names for individual bases of existential comparison/contrasts. It is in the arena of life-processes that trade-offs occur, and ASOBAT's emphasis on trade-off operations was almost overwhelming. If the role of the ASOBAT standards is one of "pointing in the desirable direction whenever a question arises as to the course that should be taken in connection with a specific problem,"[48] then the pointing is most immediately operative within the biologic processes of individuals.

Although not describable and frameable in propositions ("even if a user's decision model is known, his information requirements cannot be objectively specific"[49]), standard patterns of existential circum-

47. Committee on Managerial Decision Models, p. 47.

48. Lawrence L. Vance, "The Road to Reform of Accounting Principles," *The Accounting Review* (Oct. 1969), p. 702.

49. Joel S. Demski, "Decision-Performance Control," *The Accounting Review* (Oct. 1969), p. 670.

stances to serve as yardsticks may be tacitly known and used as comparison bases by the individuals making choices. In this context, the term "standard" is a name for the set of goal-oriented comparison/contrasts individually employed. In view of the heuristic processes involved, "relevance determination becomes a subjective issue itself."[50]

In the reaching of individual judgments about combinations and proportions of existential materials in relation to goals, trade-off is the heart of the process. "Trade-offs between [the standards] are often necessary"[51] in a contingent rather than a universal sense. Judgments of combination and proportioning of existential materials, which involve operations of comparison/contrast, could be referred to by names such as relating means/ends, quantifying, or measuring. Results of the judgmental processes could be labeled "verified," in the sense that the conclusions are currently accepted on the warrant of previously tested consequences as potentials for interactivities.

Declarations of introspective distinctions made in problem-solving situations may be publicly sharable by analogy. And actions taken in correspondence with declared distinctions serve to exemplify meanings of action terms such as relating means/ends and quantifying.

It is the process of existential discrimination, then, which may be a referent for the ASOBAT standards. The proposition that "the required degree of adherence to each standard is conditioned by the degree to which the other standards are met"[52] may be interpreted as a judgment that discriminations among space/time materials are made in reference to tacit standards relating such materials to personal goals. A "combined and simultaneous consideration of all four standards"[53] suggests reference to an environmental flux. Even the standard of relevance requires terrestrial interpretation. The Committee on External Reporting tended toward the view that discriminations or rankings of "attributes of objects or activities . . . is not possible until each attribute is identified by a specific measurement procedure."[54]

Relation of Placeholder Standards to an Encompassing Theory.— How does the interpretation of the ASOBAT standards as placeholder names for individual bases of existential discriminations relate to a guiding theory? It is possible that the ASOBAT meaning of accounting

50. Demski, "Decision-Performance Control," p. 677.
51. Committee on Managerial Decision Models, p. 47.
52. ASOBAT, p. 10.
53. ASOBAT, p. 10.
54. Committee on External Reporting, p. 92.

theory[55] is constituted by an attempted description of individuals' decision-making processes. The concepts are abstractions of assumed or observed activities and relations of wants-satisfying individuals.[56] Importantly, the abstracted concepts are available to explain specific instances of apparent decision-making.

The ASOBAT document states that the standards were "formulated by asking, 'What characteristics should accounting information have in order to be useful?' "[57] It is not strange if accounting information is deemed to possess those characteristics which an induced theory postulated for the accounting information. These would be the characteristics which accounting information "should have . . . in order to be useful." "Accounting information must be useful"[58] because usefulness is an integral part of the meaning of accounting information. "The utility of information lies in its ability to reduce uncertainty"[59] in the sense that the calorificity of heat lies in its ability to reduce unwarmth.

The warrant for action-implicated theorems of an induced theory is said to be their derivation from fundamental or realistic observational postulates. In one commentary judgment, the ASOBAT statement "differs from previous efforts in this field by placing primary emphasis on accounting standards, expressed in general terms, rather than on postulates, principles, rules or methods."[60] And it was found difficult to place the ASOBAT standards within a classification scheme for accounting postulates, especially because of an apparent overlap or lack of independence, and the failure of the ASOBAT standards "to account for all of the rational behavior" in the accounting field.[61]

Reference to a test of accounting fully for the phenomena being explained tends to confuse axiomaticizing activity with the postulational development exhibited, for example, in ARS 1. Under the present interpretation of the ASOBAT standards, they are introspective and observational postulates. Difficulties experienced by some commentators in characterizing them as generalizations of environmental observations may be related to a multiple employment of the term "standards"

55. ABSOBAT, p. 2.

56. ABSOBAT, pp. 13, 18.

57. ASOBAT, p. 3.

58. ASOBAT, p. 8.

59. ASOBAT, p. 8.

60. "Salute to the American Accounting Association," *The Journal of Accountancy* (Aug. 1966), p. 30.

61. John W. Buckley, Paul Kircher, and Russell L. Mathews, "Methodology in Accounting Theory," *The Accounting Review* (Apr. 1968), p. 276.

by a multi-oriented ASOBAT committee. In our opinion, the ASOBAT committee tacitly accepted a popular theme in accounting theory writings, that the validity of concepts is determined by their consensual abstraction from events and relations of existential environments and that a theory is sound to the extent that its component concepts describe basic, fundamental, or realistic environmental relations. In our view, this was the dominant theme of ASOBAT theory, despite notations that accounting is a measurement and communication process in some relatively modern sense.

WHAT IS THE ROLE OF THE ASOBAT STANDARDS FOR ACCOUNTANTS' USE?

Interpretation of the ASOBAT standards must take account also of the role proposed for the standards within the activities of a professional accountant class. The ASOBAT standards were ostensibly presented to an intermediary class of accountants as yardsticks for promoting inferences among existential circumstances and alternative accounting procedures. It has been noted that "the determination of 'relevant information' is left to the accountant. . . ."[62]

In presenting the standards, the ASOBAT committee could have limited its function to that of reminding about conduct of persons on the firing line of decision-making. The readers would be reminded of lessons of experience: that sound decisions involve activities of relating means to ends and that the associated measurement processes, of comparing and contrasting suggested means relative to their suitability for goal attainment, are more efficient when quantification can be employed in major degree. Alternatively, accounting researchers could be reminded that a scientific viewpoint emphasizes inquiring into expected consequences rather than concentrating on sources of being.

The role assigned to the standards was not so limited. The standards were presented to accountants, for use by accountants. And the result of their use by accountants was expected to be a pattern and content of accounting communications which reflected classification of accounting methods as acceptable or unacceptable in some functional sense.

The Accountant as Member of a Discrimination Group.—To the extent that accountants involved in internal reporting share in decision-

62. William J. Bruns, Jr., "Accounting Information and Decision-Making: Some Behavioral Hypotheses," *The Accounting Review* (July 1968), p. 477.

making problems or are in rapport with the decision-makers, they may adapt their reporting to reflect aspects of possible existential distinctions, under the label of "trade-off." Even in a context of internal accounting, however, individuals' models for selecting and processing data, reaching decisions, and taking actions are incomplete. Even the best-specified decision model will not automatically operate to discriminate among data in terms of preferable decision results.[63] Even in the context of internal reporting, "the accountant can neither objectively specify the precise information requirements of the system nor objectively evaluate the effectiveness of any specific set of information provided to the system."[64]

Professional Accountants and a PARENS PATRIAE *Function.*—The present paper is not concerned with contentions that accountants could provide users with *requested* information or otherwise perform skilled operating tasks. Even the identification of data that are common to several extant decision models has a strong taxonomic cast. The questions posed here relate to functionally significant choices.

If the standards are regarded as abstract universals, no trade-off is involved. If the standards are placeholder names for individuals' bases of comparison / contrast in assumed or observed goal-attaining behavior, the trade-offs are among existential materials and they are personal.

Yet, in the ASOBAT presentation, trade-off among the standards is an activity to be carried on by an intermediary professional class. Did the ASOBAT committee *reify* the normative concepts associable with a utilitarian view of economic activity? Is their presentation to accountants as standards for discriminatory treatment of accounting methods the reflection of a philosophic position of *conceptualism*?

Under the interpretation presented in this paper, the standards are placeholder names for individuals' comparison / contrasts which are taken to underlie observed and assumed conduct. The abstracted ideas are incorporated into a descriptive expression of individual economic behavior. The latter terms are presented to accountants not merely as clues to interpreting specific instances of apparent economic behavior. The abstracted concepts are presented as subjects amenable to existential processing under minimax principles. Determination of minimum content and best combination of the standards contained in account-

63. William H. Beaver, John W. Kennelly, and William M. Voss, "Predictive Ability as a Criterion for the Evaluation of Accounting Data," *The Accounting Review* (Oct. 1968), p. 679.

64. Demski, "Decision-Performance Control," p. 676.

ing procedures takes place within individual accountants' reasoning faculties. And it does not appear that the ASOBAT committee placed reliance on a publicly shared and grounded classification of economic objects in terms of expected objective consequences.

The purpose of this paper has been to present an interpretation of the ASOBAT standards. My task does not require that I present a substitute recommendation on standards for use by professional accountants in financial reporting. A positive statement which I might make on publicly sharable standards would be gratuitous and would be meaningful only if certain presuppositions could be shared.

It is not customary for accounting writers to disclose their assumptions about the grounds on which they expect their assertions to be accepted. This task is left to interested researchers, by default. The viewpoint that I have adopted is a naturalistic one, and it has been called a problem approach to knowledge. That position on required grounds for assertions is developed with care in John Dewey, *Logic: The Theory of Inquiry*.

The position that I have identified as dominant in ASOBAT theorization implicitly adopts a presupposition which is shared by ARS 1. That presupposition has elsewhere been labeled one-directional empiricism. An excellent example of one-directional empiricism in the field of economizing is Lionel Robbins, *The Nature and Significance of Economic Science*. Some historical notions on conceptualism and reification are collected in R. I. Aaron, *The Theory of Universals.*

Without directed attention to the conditions under which beliefs become justified through the consequences which action (directed by the beliefs) entails, the future of accounting theory holds little promise. I have chosen the course of *directed* attention.

A Response

Robert R. Sterling

PROFESSOR DEINZER begins with his characteristic thoroughness by citing some fifty-eight articles which have discussed ASOBAT.[1] The purpose of this commendable literature search is to demonstrate that there are many diverse interpretations of ASOBAT. I agree. I, too, have been struck by the number of different, sometimes contradictory, interpretations of the report. If one were to view ASOBAT as a completed theory which is supposed to provide *answers* to questions, then this would be a disturbing situation. I do not find these diverse interpretations disturbing or even surprising because I do not view ASOBAT as providing answers. Instead, I view it as asking new and different kinds of questions. In Kuhn's language, the message of ASOBAT is a new paradigm or a commitment to a new world-view. He says, "that commitment must extend to areas and to degrees of precision for which there is no full precedent. If it did not, the paradigm could provide no answers to puzzles that had not already been solved."[2] In my view, ASOBAT opens up a new line of inquiry. Like any other new line of inquiry, there are plenty of puzzles that need to be solved.

1. Harvey T. Deinzer, *Development of Accounting Thought* (New York: Holt, Rinehart and Winston, 1965).

2. Thomas S. Kuhn, *The Structure of Scientific Revolutions* (Chicago: University of Chicago Press, 1962), p. 99.

Prior to ASOBAT, there were many diverse interpretations in the literature. Since ASOBAT, there have been many diverse interpretations in the literature. The difference is only in what we are trying to interpret. Prior to ASOBAT, we were trying to define such concepts as "income," "financial position," and "unexpired cost." The literature prior to ASOBAT took the concept of, say, income as a given and then argued about how we ought to measure that concept. You will recall the lengthy and still unresolved arguments about whether LIFO or FIFO resulted in the best measure of income. You will also recall the equally lengthy and equally unresolved arguments over accelerated versus straight-line depreciation. Thus, in those days we knew *what* it was that we wanted to measure, and the arguments were concerned with *how* we were to measure the given concept. ASOBAT suggests a different line of inquiry. The relevance standard is concerned with *what* we ought to measure. If we knew which attributes were relevant, there would be no need to set up a relevance standard. Thus, the relevance standard is a question instead of an answer. It doesn't solve any problems; instead, it asks a new and different question. Given the newness of the question, I am not surprised that there are many different answers.

The notion of relevance is not new. Prior to ASOBAT, several scholars had suggested, in one form or another, that we should consider the question of relevance prior to the consideration of other questions. The thing that was new about ASOBAT was that this standard was stated *ex cathedra*. It was an official committee of the AAA that proposed this standard. Previously, the official committees of the AAA studied such specific concepts as "realization." They suggested rules for when one should realize revenue, i.e., they came up with specific measurement rules. The reasoning behind the suggested rules did not appear to be based upon relevance. ASOBAT has suggested a new line of inquiry. If we were to re-examine such questions and follow the ASOBAT suggestions, then, we would start with the question of relevance and the concept to be measured would be derived therefrom. Given that starting point, we might find that we did not need to measure realized revenue. If so, the question of how to measure it would be beside the point.

"Relevance" is an underdeveloped notion in accounting and, as we have already seen, there will be many problems in its application. However, in its general form, it seems to me that relevance is a simple and straightforward notion. All disciplines apply a standard of relevance, either implicitly or explicitly. All of the empirical sciences measure some attributes and do not measure others. Psychologists measure psychological attributes and physicists measure physical attributes. It would be odd to find a physicist administering an I.Q. test. It is not that the physicist considers I.Q. tests to be worthless or unimportant. It is simply that he finds them to be irrelevant to the problems he is concerned with. In developing his physical theories, he finds weight, volume, velocity, etc., to be relevant attributes, and he finds such things as intelligence and income measures to be irrelevant. Accountants must make the same kind of discrimination. We must decide what kinds of problems we are going to be concerned with, develop some theories for the solution of these problems, and then measure the attributes that are relevant to these theories.

In short, I think that the main message of ASOBAT is the relevance standard. To segregate attributes into relevant and irrelevant categories requires the existence of a theory. Even for a simple object, there is almost an infinite number of attributes that one could measure. Therefore, one cannot hope to measure all the attributes of any given object, and to just capriciously select certain attributes would serve no purpose. The function of a theory is, in part, to specify the attributes that are relevant. But then, there are a great many theories about a great many things. If we were to attempt to measure all the attributes specified by all the theories, we would again have an impossible task. Thus, we must select a problem area with which we wish to be concerned, and this will serve to limit the number of theories that we need be concerned with.

Perhaps an analogy would be helpful. Physicians are concerned with a great many things. The things that they are concerned with can be classified only in very general terms, i.e., "health problems." Under this general rubric, they propose and test various theories. To come upon a theory which solves a health problem is an arduous task which sometimes appears to depend as much on luck as it does on insight and intelligence. An example of this is Semmelweis' discovery of the cure for childbed fever.[3] Semmelweis tested a number of things—from the ringing of the priest's bell to vaguely defined atmospheric-cosmic-telluric changes—before he discovered the cause and cure for childbed fever. The discovery was made when one of his colleagues was accidentally nicked by a scalpel while performing an autopsy. The col-

3. Carl G. Hempel, *Philosophy of Natural Science* (Englewood Cliffs, N.J.: Prentice-Hall, 1966), pp. 3 ff.

league became ill and displayed the same kind of symptoms that were displayed by the women who had childbed fever. Semmelweis then leaped to the conclusion that there was something that got into the bloodstream that caused the malady. That is, he proposed a hypothesis or a theory which he subsequently tested and confirmed. By today's standards, his tests were crude. His measurements were even cruder. Nevertheless, his theory specified what it was that ought to be measured and controlled, albeit it was specified only in overly general terms such as "cadaveric matter." Subsequent advances in measurement methods have resulted in refinements in the theory. Conversely, subsequent advances in the theory have resulted in more specific attributes to be measured. Nowadays, measurements of such attributes are routinely made. The principle still holds: the pathologist or his laboratory technician normally measures such things as the percentage of red blood cells, but he does not normally measure the viscosity of the blood. The theory specifies that the percentage of red blood cells is relevant and that viscosity is not. These relevant attributes are then communicated to a practicing physician who makes a decision—diagnosis—based upon this information.

I propose the same kind of procedure for accounting. We can characterize the problems that we are concerned with only in the most general terms, e.g., "economic decisions." Then, we academic accountants can do research on economic decisions. We can propose theories and test them. In our quest, I expect that we will stumble and falter as much as Semmelweis did. The task is arduous. Once we have proposed and confirmed a theory, that theory will specify the relevant attributes to be measured. Then we can work on refinement of the measurement methods, which will affect the theory, and also work on refinements of the theory, which will affect what things are to be measured. The measurements routinely made by practicing accountants would be based upon the best theory available at the time.

The difficulties of this procedure are immense. In addition to the problems of research, there are political problems. If the researchers happen upon a theory which specifies a difficult measurement, they are almost certain to be told that they cannot make the measurement, because it is not objective and verifiable, or worse, because it is not generally accepted. This view inhibits progress. If medical researchers had taken this view, they could still be arguing how to measure atmospheric-cosmic-telluric changes, despite the fact that this measure is not specified by any theory. That is, it is irrelevant to everything even though it may have been generally accepted by the physicians at the time, and the measurement may have been considered objective and verifiable. For this reason, I agree with ASOBAT when it labels relevance as the *primary* standard. We must first propose and test a theory and then try to refine our method of measuring those properties that are specified by the theory. Quantifiability, freedom-from-bias, and other such standards are *secondary* considerations. General acceptance by practicing accountants is beside the point. Can you imagine a medical researcher discarding a confirmed theory because it is not generally accepted by practicing physicians? By definition, a new theory is new and therefore unknown. Therefore, the test of a new theory cannot be general acceptance.

To continue the analogy, I view the practicing accountant in the same light as the pathologist and his laboratory technicians. They routinely make the measurements that are specified by the extant theories. This does not, as some people claim, reduce the professional status of the pathologist and make him a mere bookkeeper. Difficult measurements require difficult professional judgments. This view does, however, prevent him from treating each case as if it were unique. He cannot use different measurement methods because of "differing circumstances." Each case differs in some respects, and the purpose of measurement is to discover the differences in the relevant attributes. The pathologist is not prohibited from doing research on his cases. However, he is *first* required to make the routine measurements specified by the extant theory.

The practicing physician is the receiver of the information. To communicate the relevant information to the practicing physician is not the same as making the diagnosis for him. The relevant information permits him to make a better or more-informed diagnosis. It does not guarantee that he will make the right diagnosis. The more precise the theory, the more evident the diagnosis, but, even with the relevant information, there are still a large number of judgmental diagnoses. The same is true with the receivers of accounting information. Receipt of the relevant information does not relieve the decision-maker of the task of making the decision, nor does it guarantee the right decision. Some decision models are so well specified that they can be programmed, but, even with the relevant information, most economic decisions require judgment, as well as personal preferences.

The medical researcher does not survey the practicing physicians to find out what information they want. Instead, he tries to communicate to them the advances in medical research, i.e., the confirmed new theories or the refinements in the old theories, and he tries to persuade them to use such advancements. To do otherwise would require that advances in medical theory come from the practice of medicine instead of from medical research. If medical researchers had followed this path, they would probably still be letting blood in the same way that we are still reporting sunk costs. If, as I believe, sunk costs are demonstrably irrelevant, then the fact that some decision-makers use them is not sufficient justification to continue to report them.

The above implies, and I make explicit, that I believe that there is no separate theory of accounting. Instead, there is a problem area which I prefer to call economic decisions. Researchers concerned with such problems should propose and test theories and work on refining the measurement and communication methods. Practicing accountants should routinely make the measurements that are specified by the best theory available at the time, in accordance with the best measurement methods available at the time. Then they should communicate these measurements to economic decision-makers. Thus, the practice of accounting is simply the measurement-communication function of the discipline concerned with economic decision problems. If there were a theory of accounting, it would be a theory of that function.

The impact of the message of ASOBAT is to place the burden for accounting advancements squarely where it belongs, i.e., upon the shoulders of you and me. We can no longer inventory accounting practices and then teach those practices. We can no longer try to determine the needs of the receivers by surveying them, nor can we try to justify the figures that we report by noticing that receivers use those figures. We cannot expect the APB to do the research. They are too busy with their own practice and with putting out brush fires. We academics must do the research and then try to communicate the results of that research to both practicing accountants and users of accounting information. For accounting, this is a revolutionary line of inquiry. Since it is a line of inquiry or a question instead of an answer, I am not surprised or disturbed by the diversity of opinion about the message of ASOBAT. I am only disappointed that we have, as yet, made so little progress.

The Past's Future

C. West Churchman

READING THE PAPERS to be presented at this conference was an impressive experience for me as a philosopher. It might be accurate to say the theme of the conference is as much the philosophy of accounting as it is accounting theory, since so many of the speakers have dipped into philosophical literature and philosophical concepts.

I need not apologize, therefore, because this paper also takes on so strong a philosophical tone. But, in addition to the philosophical discussion, I also have a very practical question to raise about the strategy of the practicing accountant.

My philosophical question has to deal with the role of the future in attempts to describe the past. The practical translation of this problem is the extent to which the accountant per se needs to become involved in some form of forecasting.

Common sense provides a rather ready answer to the question of the role of the future in the attempts to describe the past; the future has no role. That is to say, the practicing accountant need not concern himself with forecasting; perhaps one might want to go so far as to say that the practicing accountant, especially the CPA, is obligated to keep himself free of forecasts.

Built into this commonsense reply to the question is a preconception. Many of us have come to recognize how treacherous commonsense preconceptions can become, especially as they dig themselves like ticks into the living flesh of a scientific discipline. A student of mine has been conducting what he terms "black box experiments." The subject has a black box whose theory he is supposed to describe. He gets his information by putting four numbers into the box, then observing the four-digit output. In one of the black boxes the output is the time of day. It takes many of the subjects quite a bit of effort to realize that there is no relationship between what they are putting in and what is coming out, because the time of day is not one of their preconceptions for such a black box. This is just illustrative of the kind of fix that our preconceptions can get us into. Professors often tell their students to write down all of their preconceptions, but this piece of advice may be of little value, because if one could write down his inmost preconceptions then they would not be inmost. In this conference, however, it is possible that an outsider, joining in a serious discussion with theoreticians and practitioners, may perform some service by writing down what he observes to be some common preconceptions which seem to be the foundation of accounting theory. In a way, it is the broad task of philosophy to shatter the old tablets, so to speak. As Nietzsche said, "All the secrets of your foundation must come to light; when you are uprooted and broken in the sun, your lie will be separable from your truth."[1]

Suppose we begin with the commonsense preconception just mentioned. This is the preconception of a mind bound to the past. For such a mind, the past is sure; it is a fact, a firm foundation, value-free. The future, however, is unknown, uncertain, vague, treacherous, and threatening, and, if you wish, value-loaded. For the past-bound, we all know how we have lived. But what can we know of life in the future or life after death?

Two historical examples will suffice. David Hume in his famous treatise argues that the future is not known in the sense that direct experience is known. Indeed, from Hume's point of view, the kind of knowledge that arises from experience and memory is totally different from the kind of knowledge that is entailed in forecasting. Hume believes that it is natural for people to try to forecast. Anyone having seen a flash would expect that the noise of an explosion will occur, or having seen the heat on the stove, that it will cause a sensation of

1. F. Nietzsche, *Thus Spoke Zarathustra*, trans. M. Cowan, Gateway ed. (Chicago: Regnery Publishing Co., 1958), p. 93.

warmth. But this is expectation based on habit, and is totally different from the kind of knowledge which we acquire from observation. If we were to plot a chart in which the ordinate shows certainty and the abscissa shows time, then up to the moment of the time of the experience, there is no certainty at all. At the time of the experience, there is a sense impression, and, if it is intense enough, there is considerable certainty attached to it. After this point in time, said Hume, there will be a decay of certainty as memory enters in and begins to distort what has been directly observed.

A second example comes from the story of historical method in the nineteenth century when von Ranke made the distinction between official records, where one can obtain objectivity, and the subjective accounts of eyewitnesses and other individuals. Von Ranke was arguing that the historian's job is to sift out the subjective accounts that have no real objectivity and to devote his time to assimilating and accurately recording historical events as they are written down in various kinds of records. The similarity between von Ranke's philosophy and the one that many accountants hold seems notable. The operating statement and the balance sheet are frequently regarded as the results of the official records of the company, are carefully examined by the accountant, and are not based on subjective impressions of managers and other individuals.

In order to look carefully at the commonsense preconception that the future plays no role in the past, suppose we write out four propositions for consideration. In order to do this, we need to say something about systems and especially their components. In systems science a system is conceived as a set of components which play the role of serving the basic purposes of the whole system. In designing such systems, the systems scientist has to pay due regard to the way in which the effectiveness of one component is related to the effectiveness of another.

In the simplest case, we say that one component A is separable from another component B if the effectiveness of A does not depend in any way on the effectiveness of B. If we could write down the relationship in mathematical terms, we would say that A's effectiveness is measured by variables which are causally independent of the activities occurring in B.[2] For example, if two workers are engaged in digging a

2. The concept is often expressed by saying that the total system's separability can be represented in a linear form, i.e., as a linear function of the effectiveness of each of the components. In this regard, it should be noted that one could not

ditch, it may happen that the effectiveness of one worker is largely independent of the effectiveness of the other. Even in this simple case, however, one might suspect that pure separability does not occur. Indeed, it is safe to say that pure separability never occurs in social systems.

Now let us look at a system the purpose of which is to tell as nearly as possible the accurate story of what has happened, as well as what will happen. In such a system we could identify two activities, one of which devotes itself primarily to telling as accurately as possible what has happened (or is happening), and the other to telling what will happen.

The four propositions are the following:

1. *The activity of estimating what has happened in the past is separable from the activity of estimating what will happen in the future.* An abbreviated statement of this proposition might be, "past reckoning is separable from future reckoning."

2. *Future reckoning is separable from past reckoning.*

3. *Any specific activity of estimating what has happened in the past can be evaluated along an effectiveness scale ranging from 0 or a negative number to some maximum positive number.* In other words, this proposition states that it is possible to describe what has happened in the past, and one can do so with more or less effectiveness. The proposition does *not* state one can describe the past with complete accuracy; it only states that there is a worse and a better method of describing the past. A brief restatement would be, "knowledge of the past is possible."

4. *Knowledge of the future is possible.* Here, as in proposition 2, I have used the abbreviated form.

Now we can bring in a logician to consider our four propositions; he will tell us that these can be accepted or denied, each one in turn, and that the result of such acceptances and denials are sixteen possible positions. Thus, one can accept all four of the propositions, or one could accept the first three and deny the fourth, etc. However, there is a consideration which reduces the list of possible opinions which these four propositions express. Suppose, for example, that you believe that proposition 4 is false; that is, you do not believe that knowledge

---

arrive at such a judgment of linearity without having taken a look at the larger system and made some judgment about it. So, even in the case where the systems scientist arrives at a linear function, some nonlinearities have probably crept into his considerations.

of the future is possible. In the way in which I have expressed the meaning of proposition 4, your denial amounts to your saying that any activity involving an attempt to study the future will be absolutely ineffective. Hence, you believe there is no effectiveness measure associated with such an activity. If now we look at proposition 2, which in its complete form says that the activity of estimating what will happen in the future is separable from the activity of estimating what has happened in the past, we see that the proposition is largely meaningless if one has already accepted the idea that knowledge of the future is not possible. What the logician suggests at this point is a vacuous stipulation regarding the concept of separability, i.e., a kind of arbitrary decision as to what is to be done when an activity has no effectiveness measure associated with it. The arbitrary decision made here will be that if one argues that an activity has no effectiveness with respect to the total system, then one arbitrarily states such an activity is nonseparable from all other activities.[3]

If we make our arbitrary stipulation, it therefore follows that, if one denies proposition 4, he will also deny proposition 2. Stated otherwise, if he accepts proposition 2, he is committed to accepting proposition 4. This means that one cannot under the arbitrary stipulation consistently accept proposition 2 and deny proposition 4. Similarly, one cannot accept proposition 1 and deny proposition 3.

One final minor point rules out another two possibilities; a position which asserts that knowledge of the past is possible (accepts 3) but is nonseparable from the knowledge of the future (denies 1), and goes on to say that knowledge of the future is impossible (denies 4) would be a ridiculous position to take. A similar remark can be made for the "dual" of this in which past and future are interchanged.

What remains are seven consistent proposals as follows (we use the convention that an apostrophe after the number represents the denial of the proposition):

1, 2, 3, 4: "Separated past and future"
1, 2', 3, 4: "Forecasting from the past"
1', 2, 3, 4: "Past reckoning from the future"
1, 2', 3, 4': "Past but no future reckoning"
1', 2, 3', 4: "Future but no past reckoning"

3. The situation is very much like the one pertaining to the so-called null class in Boolean algebra, where the logician has to decide whether a class that has no members belongs or does not belong to other classes. In logic, it has been customary to say that the null class belongs to all classes; this rule produces certain conveniences in the calculus.

1', 2', 3, 4: "Integrated past and future"
1', 2', 3', 4': "Skepticism"

With appropriate apologies for this logical exercise, suppose now we examine these seven consistent statements, or rather, all of them except the last. I assume that in this audience there can be no real interest in skepticism, because, if one were to adopt it, the whole activity of the accounting profession becomes a kind of sardonic joke.

In this examination, as I hinted at the beginning, I would like to take both an epistemological and a strategic look at the propositions. By a strategic look, I mean that a practitioner might agree, for example, that the future can be predicted, but assert that it is none of his business to predict it. I gather this feeling has entered into some of the policies regarding CPA's. I will be interested in both the epistemological and the strategic discussion of the propositions.

At the outset I mentioned what I thought would be a common preconception; namely, that one could tell the past but one could not tell the future, or strategically it is none of his business to tell the future. This is expressed in the fourth of the list of positions which I have dubbed "Past but no future reckoning." It is a series of propositions that has often been accepted by strong positivists, or individuals in disciplines like history who have felt that man can know what his past has been like, but is completely incapable of predicting the future even approximately. We'll see as we progress in the discussion that this particular piece of common sense has many shades of meaning.

The opposite of the commonsense position is the one I have called "Future but no past." This says that one can tell very well what is going to happen, but one cannot tell what did happen. For example, a man whose wife has just told him that she is going to divorce him and marry the iceman believes he can predict what will happen, but does not have any idea what did happen. However, there is no discipline of science that I know of which would accept this combination of assertions and denials. The past has always been such a fundamental part of scientific inquiry that to deny the possibility of saying anything sensible about it would seem to aim at the very heart of the scientific method itself.

The position, however, that I want to argue most strongly for, and which is the deadly enemy of the commonsense preconception, is the one called "Integrated past and future." This position, too, has many different shades of meaning, depending on how the future enters into the determination of the past. I want to give its strongest possible meaning, and for this purpose I will turn to operations research.

Professor Chambers in his paper makes a distinction between a report and a physical fact. He illustrates this in the case of inventory, where, he says, the report contains the items described by numbers, whereas the physical facts are the items actually in inventory that can be observed. From this illustration one might infer, as did Hume in the discussion above, that the direct observation of the physical condition of inventory is more reliable than the report, the report corresponding to Hume's term "decay in memory."

But the question that faces the operations researcher is the meaning of "reliable." The operations researcher's task is to assist the decision-maker in controlling inventory; he will do this by trying to decide on the optimal amounts to be ordered into inventory at various points of time.

Now what are the appropriate data that the operations researcher should use in making his study in order to assist the decision-maker? An obvious reply to this question, a reply that is contained in many operations research texts, is to say that the operations researcher should examine past invoices. The student is told to make a frequency chart, using certain intervals of time, e.g., a day, a week, or a month. This provides the basis of his inferring the probability distribution of demand on inventory. He is also cautioned to observe trends in time, e.g., seasonal fluctuations or gradually rising or falling sales demand and to extrapolate into the future on the basis of these trends.

These recommendations to the operations research student, in fact, are based on what I labelled "Future reckoning from the past," i.e., the recommendations are based on the assumption that past reckoning is independent of future reckoning but not vice versa. But a moment's reflection shows the weakness of this position. Suppose, for example, that there is a seasonal fluctuation of demand. Then it may be very sensible during the off-season to reduce prices and increase advertisement in order to smooth the demand curve. If this were done, then obviously the use of very careful statistical analysis of past data and an extrapolation of seasonal fluctuations into the future would be largely irrelevant because a new kind of demand system would have been created. In the language of systems science discussed above, it is quite obvious that the demand system is not separable from the inventory system. If one does use past demand and makes the kinds of extrapolations mentioned above, he is making a very strong systemic judgment, namely, that nothing can be changed about the demand system, e.g., because the managers are reluctant to make such changes or else because the customers are fixed in their patterns of purchasing.

The same remarks apply to the determination of cost by operations researchers. Obviously, in the case of inventory, it is necessary to determine the cost of holding items in inventory. This cost is an opportunity cost. It is an inference as to how a dollar released from inventory could best be spent in some other activity of the firm. Opportunity costs are what some philosophers of science call "counterfactual conditionals."[4] The counterfactual conditional has the form, "If X were to occur, then Y would occur." In the case of the cost of holding inventory, for example, the counterfactual conditional is "If inventory were to be reduced by such and such an amount, then the released funds could optimally be used to yield P percent return." It is to be noted that the demand on inventory is also an opportunity demand, i.e., based on counterfactual conditional of the form, "If such and such were to be done to the demand system, then the demand function would be so and so."

What is it that the operations researcher observes in order to provide information for decision-making purposes? We have heard a good deal at this conference about how information should be generated for decision-making, so that the question is quite relevant: what does one observe in order to verify a counterfactual conditional? At first glance, the problem seems impossible to solve; how can I observe anything in order to judge what would happen (but never does)? This is why Goodman uses the term "counterfactual." Their premises never, in fact, occur in nature. So it begins to appear as though operations researchers must be spinning their wheels.

But the situation is not hopeless. If one were willing to make a judgment about the future of the whole system, then on the basis of this judgment he would be justified in using a certain kind of data. Suppose, for example, that one makes a judgment that nothing can be changed about the demand system. Then, on the basis of this judgment and the additional judgment that the system will exist in essentially the same environment as it has in the past, one would be justified in taking past invoices and performing the exercise specified above, i.e., extrapolating into the future and using these extrapolations as the basis for calculating optimal inventory policy. In other words, if a strong sys-

4. See Nelson Goodman, *Fact, Fiction and Forecast* (Cambridge, Mass.: Harvard University Press, 1955).

temic judgment is made, then a certain kind of data bank, based on past observation, can be said to be authorized. If no systemic judgment seems sensible to make, then of course the operations researcher must regard the problem as intractable.

We see that information for decision-making is really a compound of at least two kinds of activities: the one concerned with *authorizing* a certain set of data for use on the analysis and the other in the collection of the data itself. But the authorization procedure is essentially a forecast about the future, because it makes a judgment about the characteristics the system will or would have. It is, in fact, much more than a simple forecast, because it must be a model which permits one to say what would happen if certain things were to occur. In this regard the systemic judgment is much more like a set of differential equations in physics, where the boundary conditions can be changed and one can infer which events would occur under these changes.

It is clear that the authorization of a data bank is future reckoning. We can now understand how past reckoning is inseparable from future reckoning, because we need to make very strong and effective judgments about the future in order to be able to use the past effectively. I might add that the reverse is also clear; that is to say, effective reckoning of the past is essential, because effective judgments about the future of the system must somehow draw on past experience. Hence, future reckoning is nonseparable from past reckoning, and vice versa. From these remarks we can conclude that the operations researcher must adopt the position I labelled "Integrated past and future."

What relevance has all of this discussion for the accountant? At this conference we have been swinging between two positions: the one in which there is chiefly a concern with the practicing accountant and his problems of collecting information and the other with the broader question of the accountant as an information collector and as an aid to the decision-maker. I would say that the distinction between the two positions is essentially the strategic question as to whether or not the accountant should be involved in what I called authorization of data banks, i.e., whether the accountant should be involved in the very difficult problem of making adequate systemic judgments. One might adopt the position that the accountant essentially gathers the data, and the authorization is made by the managers or by the legal system. This position would argue for a separability of the information system from the decision-making system, where the accountant does one kind of job and the managers or lawyers do the other kind of job. I think the position is undoubtedly weak in terms of system design. But the real issue depends, so to speak, on the ambition of the accounting profession. Does it wish to become involved in authorizing data banks and hence in making strong systemic judgments?

I have argued elsewhere[5] that information becomes measurement if the information is widely usable in a variety of contexts. I gather from some of the papers in this conference, e.g., Sprouse and Rappaport, that at least some accountants do regard their data in terms of the user and his characteristics and are seeking to make accounting a measurement process. If so, then I would infer that these accountants are strongly involved in considerations of the authorization of data banks based on strong systemic judgments.

In concluding, I would like to make several general remarks about the "Integrated past and future" position. We are going through an age where we are reconsidering many of our traditional human values. From the point of view of the science of the last century, precision, rigor, and clarity were desiderata. The scientist, it was believed, should become clear and precise about his position, and his position should essentially be a consistent one. These values led the scientists to regard descriptions of the past in terms of the "quality of the reports." Reports should be specific, concrete, and unobjectionable. According to this past value system, when we look at the most vital event in the life of a company, namely a sale, one would tend to regard dollar amount and quantity ordered as representing the highest quality a report can attain. We note, however, in terms of our earlier discussion, that the quality of being clear and precise may be at variance with the quality of best serving the user. What does the stockholder think when he reads the item "gross sales"? If he is sensible, he will wonder "What might sales have been?" He is, indeed, raising the counterfactual question again. And the answer to his question must be based on a strong systemic judgment, which, I believe, will inevitably be ambiguous, not clear and precise, and certainly not unobjectionable. We live in a world where we have to make strong systemic judgments in order to make our decisions, but if we are honest we will see that we will forever fail to find the unobjectionable basis for these systemic judgments that authorize the use of certain data banks. So the quality of the report as a concept has changed in terms of a new set of values.

5. C. West Churchman, *Prediction and Optimal Decision* (Englewood Cliffs, N.J.: Prentice-Hall, 1961).

On the positive side, this new set of values represents a willingness to be as honest as possible about the basis of our decision-making. Along with this willingness goes, by necessity, the need to accept ambiguity, vagueness, and incomplete consensus as essential qualities of our reports.

I would like to close with a very general philosophical opinion, about which I hope there will be considerable debate, for debate is the essence of everything I have discussed in terms of systemic judgment.

I realize, as Norton Bedford has, that we have been developing a culture which pays more and more respect to the future—to what it will be or should be—in 1984, 2000, or 10,000. But in this paper I have really been putting in a plea for our respect to the past, to what it was and might have been. It is really quite disrespectful for us to assume that the past was simple and easy to describe. What was it like to be alive in the year 1800? No amount of historical data could possibly probe the depth and complexity of such a question. The past is as deep an uncertainty and ambiguity as is the future.

While I appreciate the urge for accounting to limit and define its task, I also appreciate the need for it to expand its horizons and to identify its allies who are all those who are devoting their lives to the worship of the past. There was a time when basic science regarded itself as one form of the adoration of God. The ritual of this form of worship of God by worshipping the past entails the enormous and heroic task of telling the future.

Discussion of "The Past's Future"

Robert E. Jensen

SEVERAL DAYS prior to this theory symposium, I received a letter from Professor Churchman containing a brief sketch of his thoughts on the paper which he intended to prepare for the symposium at the University of Florida on March 13, 1970. My following discussion of his presentation, which was also delivered at that time, is given below. Most portions of this discussion remain relevant to Professor Churchman's revised paper written subsequent to the symposium.

In his letter, Professor Churchman states: "I'll try to give you the basic idea of my remarks, and perhaps I can fill you in on further details when we meet in Gainesville." I am grateful for his letter, since it does allow me to prepare this discussion paper in advance of Professor Churchman's delivery of the completed paper. If my remarks are somewhat incoherent, two major reasons are (1) that Professor Churchman's letter is vague in places; and (2) other commitments and logistic constraints in preparing these comments for distribution allowed brief time for both planning and writing before my departure for Florida—and those hours were plagued by interruptions.

Although I am not a philosopher, my comments suffer from the philosopher's vices of verbalism and idle speculation. Professor Churchman states four propositions and then seems to appeal for us to assert or deny that each proposition holds in accounting. Of course, we cannot assert or deny anything for *all* accounting since we do not know what comprises all past and future accounting.

One approach might be to mentally construct accounting rules based upon certain assumptions and then to prove or disprove the four propositions in the language of tautologies. This philosophy dates back at least as far as Plato, with Aristotle becoming the best-known father of the scholastic view that all problems can be solved by the operations of pure thinking.

Given the appropriate axioms concerning a triangle, we may prove that the sum of its angles is equal to two right angles. However, what does the above proof have as a referent in the real world? Perhaps no triangular object in the physical world can satisfy the rigorous requirements of a triangle in Euclidean geometry; certainly *all* triangular objects do not satisfy such requirements. Similarly, perhaps no accounting practice would conform to any axiomatic accounting system.

In attempting to determine how the various parts of a system and its environment are interrelated, management scientists (or systems analysts) often encounter tremendous difficulties caused by lack of data. Sometimes data are not available, merely because the need was not previously foreseen. In other instances, existing information systems have been myopic and entrenched in traditionalism to such an extent that innovation in ways of measuring things has not kept pace with advances in electronic technology for transmitting, storing, and processing information. Other problems are created by the lack of centralized control over information-gathering among the various parts of a system and its environment.

Management scientists have been among the most vocal critics of accounting systems, which rarely are able to supply systems measurements needed in decision-model formulation and usage. But, aside from many superficial and misleading claims, these scientists have fared little better than accountants in solving these information problems; i.e., we are still awaiting significant breakthroughs in coming to practical grips with realistic problems.

The mathematical models which the management scientist has developed some expertise in forming and solving are either deterministic or probabilistic, with implicit stationarity assumptions. In practice he finds that stationarity conditions are seldom realistic. The system and its environment are constantly changing.

In college the would-be scientist discovers that one of the advantages of many types of management-science models (e.g., linear programming models) is that they provide opportunity-cost measures. In practice he later discovers that he is no better able to measure the most relevant opportunity costs than the accountant who readily admitted that such costs were not measurable because of difficulties in identifying *all* lost opportunities, uncertainties, and contingencies concerning events inside and outside the system under different conditions over time, inability to identify the true system, etc. Churchman recognizes this in an excellent book entitled *The Systems Approach*. With reference to the management scientist, he states: "We see again the kink in our hero's armor: he seems tied to the particular system he is studying and must allow some other form of 'non-scientific' or even 'nonsystematic' judgment to take over when the issues go beyond the system to which he is shackled."[1]

The problem in supplying relevant information in systems analysis is that the systems of major interest are comprised of human beings. Research problems are the same as those encountered in the social sciences. Unlike physical and natural scientists, social scientists are seldom able to get beyond the stage of identifying correlations in social phenomena; i.e., cause/effect relationships tend to be much more complex, elusive, and unstable than their counterparts studied by physical and natural scientists.

With these points in mind, let me proceed to several specifics in Professor Churchman's proposed discussion in this symposium.

(1) Concepts of past and future are not entirely clear to me. In one sense the past, P_0, may be viewed as an *entire set* of experiences which affect the behavior (including thinking) of an observer.[2] The future, F_0, in this context becomes the set of all other (potential) experiences not contained in P_0, as shown in the Venn diagram on page 152. An all-knowing being, God, in this case has no future, i.e., $P_0 = \Omega_0$ by virtue of the fact that he is all-knowing.

But the past may be comprised of more than just human experiences for those who believe that trees fall in forests and stars are formed irrespective of human awareness of such phenomena. It might be help-

1. C. West Churchman, *The Systems Approach* (New York: Delacorte Press, 1968), p. 72.

2. Previous thought processes may of course generate experiences apart from experiences received through sensory receptors. In addition, in human beings, as well as other animals, there may be instincts or unconscious experiences resulting from genetic or chemical processes which affect behavior. Their internal thoughts also become experiences.

ful at this point to distinguish sets of past and potential future experiences (P_o and F_o) of an observer and past and future actual events (P_e and F_e) which take place whether experienced or not by the observer. Events succeed each other as a manifold of distinct points along a continuous time scale. An all-knowing being, God, in this case may have a future in the sense that at any point t in time, the set F_e of future events is comprised of all events that occur subsequent to time t whether predetermined or not. Obviously, some elements of P_o and F_o

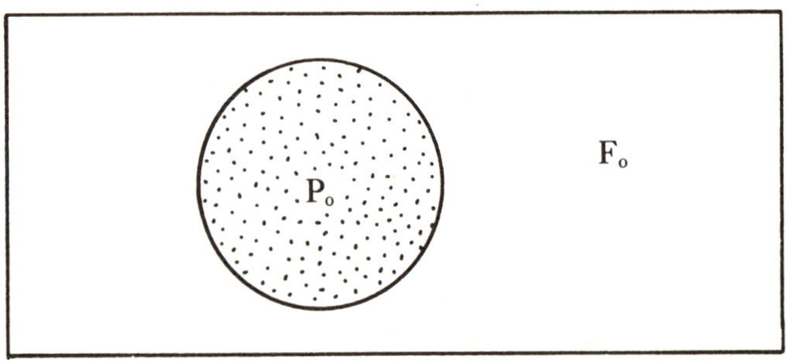

$$\Omega_o = P_o + F_o$$

may be contained in P_e and F_e, since human experiences are also events. However, F_o may, in addition, be comprised of possible human experiences which never do eventually occur.

For illustrative purposes, consider a scientist awaiting the delivery of a rock specimen being collected at time t by the first astronauts walking on the moon's surface. The formation of this rock resulted from a subset of actual past events $p_e \in P_e$ which took place prior to time t. The subsequent return of the specimen to earth, the recovery of the space capsule, etc., were among the subset $f_e \in F_e$ of future events which eventually unfolded subsequent to time t. The scientist's possible future sensations of experiencing that the rock has a granular texture were contained in the subset $f_o \in F_o$. These future experiences need not eventually be realized; e.g., the texture may not be granular.

Human awareness of actual past events, we will assume, results only from human experiences. The record of the event is usually accepted as more official when care is taken to reduce distortion in sensory perceptions and / or many people agree that their experiences of the event were identical or sufficiently comparable.

(2) We may consider what Professor Churchman has in mind when he refers to "activities of estimating" the past and future. With respect to personal past and future experiences, these activities might be viewed as functions π_o and φ_o, where

$$\hat{p}_o = \pi_o(P_o);$$
$$\hat{f}_o = \varphi_o(\hat{p}_o).$$

For example, $\hat{p}_o$ might denote the scientist's estimation of a subset $p_o \epsilon P_o$ that he has experienced from past courses, reading, thoughts, and experiments relevant to moon rock analyses. In this case, $\hat{p}_o$ need not be identical to p_o, because of memory lapses concerning his actual experiences, subconscious experiences which he does not consciously recall, etc. The subset $\hat{f}_o$ might be viewed as an estimate of $f_o \epsilon F_o$ of his future experiences when eventually analyzing the specimen.

The activities of estimating the past and future may also concern actual events in time. These activities might be defined as π_e and φ_e functions, where

$$\hat{p}_e = \pi_e(\hat{p}_o);$$
$$\hat{f}_e = \varphi_e(\hat{p}_o).$$

In this case $\hat{p}_o$ denotes all past experience consciously involved in the estimating activities. For instance, the scientist's activity of estimating what physical events $p_e \epsilon P_e$ in the past caused the formation of the moon rock consists of evaluating all recollected experiences (learning), $\hat{p}_o$, to arrive at an estimate, p_e, of $\hat{p}_e$; i.e., he forms the hypothesis $p_e = \hat{p}_e$. He doesn't know how or when the rock was actually formed, but he nevertheless makes his $\hat{p}_e$ estimate of p_e. At subsequent points in time new experiences may lead to new estimates. Conversely, $\hat{f}_e$ is a subset of his predicted future events, e.g., predicted future astronaut landings on more distant bodies in outer space. The φ_e function consists of forming such predictions as extrapolations of his previous learning experience.

(3) The concept of "separable" in Professor Churchman's propositions 1 and 2 is also confusing to me. Separability may be defined in terms of some criterion or variable; e.g., two things may be separable in space but not separable in time and vice versa. Professor Churchman discusses the term "separable" in the context of independence and systems effectiveness; i.e., two components of a system are separable if their contributions to total system effectiveness are independent.

But in failing to define "independent" and "total system effectiveness," he fails to adequately define "separability." For example, can two things be separable without a measure of effectiveness? Can there be more than one criterion of system effectiveness, and if so, can two components then be separable according to certain criteria and not separable according to other criteria? Suppose proposition 3 is denied; i.e., the activity of estimating what has happened in the past *cannot* be evaluated along an effectiveness scale. Does this render meaningless the concept of separability in propositions 1 and 2?

Suppose for the moment that a measure of effectiveness, $m(\pi_e,\varphi_e)$, exists as a function of activities of estimating both past and future. Further, assume that the contributions of each component to m are additive; i.e.,

$$m(\pi_e,\varphi_e) = g(\pi_e) + h(\varphi_e).$$

The activity components π_e and φ_e are separable in terms of Professor Churchman's criterion; whereas, they are not separable if

$$m(\pi_e,\varphi_e) = g(\pi_e)h(\varphi_e).$$

However, in either case the measure of effectiveness m is predicated upon existence of both π_e and φ_e; i.e., the measure of effectiveness assumed by Professor Churchman (in defining separability of activities of estimating past and future events) cannot be obtained unless both activities take place. The only exception would be where the measure of effectiveness is independent of a given activity; e.g.,

$$\begin{aligned} m(\pi_e,\varphi_e) &= g(\pi_e)+0\varphi_e \\ &= g(\pi_e). \end{aligned}$$

This, however, is a more restrictive concept of independence than is implied by Professor Churchman. Also note that, if his proposition 1 (or 2) is asserted, then his proposition 3 (or 4) cannot be denied; i.e., if π_e and φ_e are separable in terms of $m(\pi_e,\varphi_e)$, then the π_e and φ_e activities can be evaluated in terms of their additive contributions $g(\pi_e)$ and $h(\varphi_e)$ to total system effectiveness.

Subject to the possibility of an incorrect interpretation of propositions 1 and 2, suppose we restate them as

(1) π_e does not entail φ_e,
(2) φ_e does not entail π_e.

For instance, proposition 1 now states that the activity of estimating what events have occurred in the past is possible even when the activity of estimating future events does not take place. These propositions no longer assume the existence of a single measure of effectiveness or exclude the existence of various measures of effectiveness. Either proposition may be denied for reasons other than nonadditivity of π_e and φ_e contributions to a single criterion.

(4) The accountant accounts for a system's financial performance over time periods and the financial position at the end of each period. Events of interest in this process are exchange transactions (between the system and its environment and between components within the system). In this context, consider proposition 1 in the form

$$\pi_e \text{ does not entail } \varphi_e;$$

e.g., the activity of estimating past exchange transactions does not entail the activity of estimating future transactions.

One type of transaction which might be illustrated here is the outflow of resources for income tax. Let π_e denote the activity of estimating or computing the tax paid (or due) on past transactions. Interestingly, there are many provisions in the tax law which require the activity of estimating future events in computing the tax. For instance, depreciation is required for many types of fixed assets, where the allowable depreciation methods entail the activity of estimating future usage (i.e., useful life) and future salvage value. In other words, an activity of estimating the tax due on past operations requires by law the activity of estimating certain future operations.

Next, consider proposition 2 in the form

$$\varphi_e \text{ does not entail } \pi_e;$$

e.g., the activity of estimating future exchange transactions of the system does not entail the activity of estimating past transactions. Previously, the activities of estimating fixed asset usage (economic life) and future salvage value were mentioned. Accounting practices in this regard involve revising estimates of economic life and salvage value, if original estimates are out of line because of unexpected physical changes in the asset (e.g., damage by fire or major improvements), changes in salvage market conditions, etc. Clearly, the activities of estimating economic life and salvage value in practice do entail the activity of estimating past events.

Many other examples exist in accounting where basic transactions entail the activities of estimating both past and future events. Hence, propositions 1 and 2 must, in my viewpoint, be denied for at least some accounting activities. However, their denial is hardly enlightening. Even the most conservative accountants admit having to estimate future events in setting bad debt allowances, allocating period costs, valuing inventories, setting up contingency reserves, etc.

In other words, I disagree with Professor Churchman's contention that most accounting theorists would assert proposition 1. Even the accountant in a simple cash-basis accounting system, whose sole function is one of recording cash inflows and outflows of the firm, must estimate future events (or rely on estimates of others), e.g., in computing taxes when tax depreciation is mandatory. In accrual accounting systems, which are much more prevalent, activities of estimating both past and future operations are required.

(5) In his letter Professor Churchman suggested that the assertion of proposition 1 and denial of proposition 2 were implicit in the ethical policies of auditors. Of major concern to auditors is the valuation of a firm's assets. The general basis of valuation is historical cost, derived from examining past transactions. However, the doctrine of conservatism prevails; i.e., the auditor is to ascertain that reported historical cost valuation is not materially in excess of market value. But, appraisals to determine market value usually entail the activity of estimating events in the future. Thus, whether the auditor performs the appraisal or whether he relies on outside appraisals, he cannot disassociate himself from estimates of the future. Many other instances arise where auditors must ethically look to the future.

The more relevant question is why does the accountant report certain future estimates and not others in external reports to the investing public. For example, why does the doctrine of conservatism prevail? Why does the auditor write down asset values if predictions are gloomy but not write them up from historical values when predictions are rosy?

Such inconsistencies in allowing forecasts and predictions to affect accounting reports have been the focus of endless debate (which I will not delve into here). Suffice it to say that this remains an enigma to those who attempt to make categorical statements about accounting. *But then this is only one of many types of inconsistencies that can be found in accounting.*

(6) Professor Churchman seems to favor the denial of propositions

1 and 2. For reasons alluded to previously, I agree that particular instances were encountered or can be conceived in which activities of estimating past and future events cannot be decoupled. However, I am also uncomfortable about denying these propositions for all activities in general. Does the scientist really have to estimate future events when engaged in the activity of estimating what events millions of years ago took place when the moon was formed? Does the accountant have to estimate what transactions will occur in the future while recording cash sales receipts?

In any case, it becomes an empirical problem in determining what constitutes the activity of estimating in each case. Suppose it is found that A ignored the future when estimating events of the past, whereas B looked ahead as well. It might be asserted that A, nevertheless, made certain implicit assumptions concerning the future; this points out some subtle definitional problems in distinguishing activities of estimating past and future events.

(7) The relationship between Professor Churchman's propositions 3 and 4 and propositions 1 and 2 is also confusing to me. The only distinction between propositions 3 and 4 concerns the activity of estimating the past (proposition 3) versus the activity of estimating the future (proposition 4). *However, denial of propositions 1 and 2, that these two activities are independent, seems to render meaningless the distinction between propositions 3 and 4.* Apart from this, the phrasing of propositions 3 and 4 leads us into endless philosophical questions. E.g., what are measures of effectiveness? What constitutes event relationships? What is knowledge?

(8) Professor Churchman argues in effect that if a group of persons are to agree that certain events have truth or falsity requires "not only linguistic standards of communications, but a calibration procedure." This raises some paradoxical questions. For example, can persons without any form of calibration procedure distinguish between truth and falsity of an event; e.g., can primitive natives recognize that the sun did momentarily disappear in a total solar eclipse, or must they await computer reports compiled by scientists in their village who carefully calibrated movements of the sun, moon, and earth? Suppose the natives all agree that the sun which they see following the eclipse is not the same sun which they saw prior to the darkness—is this a true event for them?

The main difference between the scientists and the natives is that the natives in and of themselves probably could not predict the place, time, and duration of a solar eclipse; whereas, scientists predicted the event hundreds of years previous to direct human experiencing of the phenomenon. The aim of all science is to predict, and herein lies the value of a calibration procedure. The scientist, in a repetitive process, seeks to identify relationships between changes in phenomena. The finer his calibrations, the more the world of change is visible to him.

Discovered relations provide clues of more complex interrelationships. The scientist is not content merely to identify correlation. Science is an inductive process which entails sentences of the form X″ follows from X′. Theories are formed by mental processes. Imprecise structures are often made more exact by formalization of axiomatic assumptions, derivation of definitions of basic concepts, and performance of tautological transformations to derive conclusions that are tested by new empirical operations. No theory is final; all are subject to new testing and subsequent revision. In this process the scientist must estimate the future in order to form his theories and efficiently create the appropriate experimental conditions in which to make new observations.

(9) In discussing propositions 3 and 4, Professor Churchman seems to be appealing for greater quantification. I am inclined to agree, although some analysts might argue that qualitative evaluation has not received sufficient attention. David Novick, for example, stated: "Between profit budgeting in private industry and Mr. McNamara's cost effectiveness in the military world, I wonder if we are not going a little berserk on the quantity concept. There are many things that can be quantified. I think what we are losing sight of, in this era of the computer and the network context and the rest of it, is that there can be a lot of very important and significant qualitativeness."[3]

But the accountant, particularly the managerial accountant, should be mainly concerned with that aspect of management where a decision must be made from among two or more alternatives. In ultimately choosing an alternative, the manager must, at that point where the buck finally stops, quantify effectiveness in criteria or goal attainment on at least an ordinal scale in order to conclude that the chosen alternative is better than or as good as all other alternatives. This holds even for criteria reflected as constraints rather than in the objective function. For instance, suppose the manager absolutely does not want effect E. The model builder may now ordinally code this criterion by

3. Cyril O'Donnell, ed., *The Strategy of Corporate Research* (San Francisco: Chandler Publishing Co., 1967), p. 94.

saying that not-E is better than E. All alternatives with E may then be eliminated by imposing a constraint to that effect.

In this regard, the manager differs from humanists, art critics, etc., who perform qualitative evaluations without necessarily having to make forced-choice decisions.

When a literature professor, for example, reads novel D by Dostoevski and play I by Ibsen, he may qualitatively evaluate for his entire life what he has drawn from both D and I as a literary critic. If, on the other hand, he must choose one or the other for the university library (which cannot purchase both due to a budgetary restraint), the professor becomes more than a critic. He now becomes a manager or decision-maker, who must in effect implicitly quantify his analysis in deciding whether D is better than, as good as, or worse than I for purposes of library acquisition.

(10) The above illustration of the literature professor also indicates what an almost hopeless task it is in certain decision settings to identify the relevant criteria upon which to measure effectiveness of an activity. One problem is that the professor himself may not be able to spell out or communicate all the criteria which he used and how he related these criteria to D and I in reaching his decision. Thus, the management scientist, in attempting to build a model of this decision process, becomes impeded in identifying the relevant criteria upon which he would like to attempt to measure the effectiveness of library holdings of D and I.

Professor Churchman touches upon a similar point when suggesting that social damage of alcoholism might be quantitatively measured as lost days of work. He then states: "The suggested measure of merit of the mission has much of the 'nonhuman' if not 'inhuman,' attitude of the management scientist at work. The main point about alcoholism for the humanist is the heartaches of a family brought about by an alcoholic parent. Actually, many an alcoholic can earn a living satisfactorily enough, but his evenings of drunkenness produce the family tragedy. There are the moralists, besides, who see in alcoholism a breakdown of personal morality, which occurs whether or not the individual misses a day's work."[4] Nevertheless, even the humanist or the moralist, when placed in a position to decide whether alcohol is to be legally prohibited or not, must translate qualitative effects such as family tragedy and breakdown of personal morality into quantitative terms when he subjectively concludes that legal prohibition is better

4. Churchman, *The Systems Approach*, p. 85.

than, as good as, or worse than no legal prohibition, assuming he is convinced that prohibition will have some effect upon alcoholism. But he may not be able to reveal to the model builder the criteria and the implicit weightings of these criteria which led to his decision.

The point I am trying to make here is that, in seeking to measure effectiveness, it is first necessary to determine effectiveness *on what*, i.e., effectiveness relative to a specific criterion or goal. Unfortunately, relevant criteria buried deep within human feelings cannot be easily identified even though their quantification is implicitly assumed whenever a human decision-maker makes a choice. The humanist contends that the capacity for human feeling is infinite and that particular feelings are temporal. Hence, he concludes that the scientist, in attempting to measure such things, has embarked upon a task which is not only futile at any point in time but meaningless over time.

Professor Churchman asserts that "all efforts to ascertain the truth or falsity of an event for a group of persons spread out over time and space requires not only linguistic standards of communication, but a calibration procedure." In this regard, we might note a statement by von Mises: "In the works of poetry, fine arts, music, etc. general contents of experience, condensed into moods and feelings, are communicated by means of special 'languages,' whose conventions are assimilated in education and instruction. None of these contents can be translated without loss from one language into another one. We do not know of an objective definition of the 'beautiful' independent of the apprehending subject. A scientific theory, as well as a work of art, is always a one-sided hint to possible experiences, never their complete exhaustion."[5] One advantage of a calibration procedure lies in its ability to be "translated without loss from one language to another one." But, the experiencing of an event by the individual, may, nevertheless, be true for an individual and extend well beyond the scientist's ability to calibrate.

(11) In propositions 3 and 4 we are concerned with calibration, which in turn purportedly requires a theory of causal linkage. At a recent colloquium Professor Churchman presented the argument that social scientists have misguided themselves concerning causality:

> To state the point of view in another way, in the physical science model, the physicist must necessarily bring in a presuppo-

5. Richard von Mises, *Positivism* (New York: Dover Publications, 1951), p. 370.

> sition about a causal linkage between events which he observes. Without such a causal linkage, he could not possibly do a proper job of calibration and instrumentation.
>
> Many social scientists, on the other hand, show a great reluctance to make any kind of causal assumption about the world until evidence for causality has been developed through the data. But the argument given above shows that in fact they do make causal assumptions implicitly.
>
> Once we recognize that the process of data collection requires an *a priori* causal theory, then the debate about inferring causal links by means of statistical regression theory becomes futile.[6]

It seems that he overstates his case in this situation, e.g., by suggesting that "inferring causal links by means of statistical regression theory becomes futile." Suppose, for example, that the search for DDT in sea and bird life really originated as a result of an accidental discovery of a correlation between the increased use of the pesticide and decreased numbers of fish and fowl or increased numbers of infertile eggs. Such a discovery might have prompted chemical investigations which ultimately disclosed a causal linkage between DDT usage and death or infertility of wildlife. Medical history is filled with accounts of situations where important discoveries originated with quite accidental observations of relationships between variables. Are we to reduce the chances for such accidental discoveries in the social sciences by discrediting efficient empirical techniques (e.g., statistical regression analysis) for discovering correlations between variables?

In addition, it is questionable whether the physical scientist always presupposes a "causal linkage between events which he observes." Bunge, for instance, notes that: "There are many ways of understanding, that is, of understanding why-questions, the disclosure of causes being but one of such ways. . . . Causality is not a sufficient condition for understanding reality, although it is quite often a component of scientific explanation. . . . Scientific explanation is, in short, explanation by laws—not necessarily explanation by causes."[7] For example, Newton's second law of motion reads

$$ma = kF,$$

6. C. West Churchman, "The Systems Approach to Measurement in Business Firms," paper presented at Accounting Colloquium I, University of Kansas School of Business, April 24–26, 1969, p. 5.

7. Mario Bunge, *Causality* (Cambridge, Mass.: Harvard University Press, 1959), pp. 305–6.

where a constant k multiplied by force F is equal to the product of mass m multiplied by its acceleration a. Among other things, the law is useful in explaining movements of bodies in space. But this does not mean that any one part of the equation *causes* the other. Rosenberg, in an excellent recent work, contends that "We speak of a cause when an external influence produces a change in some unit. The term 'produces' is crucial in this definition, for it implies that an efficient, external agent exercises an isolable power on the unit. Causes have properties of uniqueness, isolability, productiveness, in variability, unidirectionality, etc., which are by no means characteristic of many asymmetrical relationships in social science."[8]

The major difficulty in the social sciences usually lies in the inability to follow up a discovered relationship with controlled experimentation found in the physical and biological sciences. For example, the effects of DDT in wildlife reproduction can be experimentally studied under conditions where the presence or absence of DDT is the only major factor which varies under experimental conditions. In studying the effects of poverty on the divorce rate, it is difficult to achieve controlled experimentation which isolates poverty as a contributing factor from other major factors affecting human behavior (e.g., race, religion, intelligence, education, legal environment, drinking, occupation, nutrition).

Still another problem in the social sciences is that the systems under study are typically much less stable than in the physical and biological sciences. For example, suppose we could experimentally study the effects on Canadian government attitudes concerning drainage of polluted waters flowing into Canada from United States border areas. This might be of little value, not only because human attitudes are volatile and subject to rapid change, but also because the Canadian government itself does not remain constant; e.g., deaths and elections frequently change representatives at the various levels of government. Effects of DDT on the reproductive systems of fish and fowl, on the other hand, do not present such a problem to chemists and biologists, because reproductive systems in different animals of a given species are much less variable than human attitudes of different people and at different times.

Still another problem in the social sciences is that mere discovery of certain relationships in a system may affect the system in and of itself.

8. Morris Rosenberg, *The Logic of Survey Analysis* (New York: Basic Books, 1970), p. 10.

For example, suppose a study reveals how a particular operating manager behaves under certain conditions. The manager, for any one of various possible reasons, may accordingly change his behavior to make it less predictable. Clarkson, for instance, conducted an extensive study of a trust investor's decision process in portfolio selection.[9] This enabled Clarkson to simulate this process in a computer model which, for several clients, selected portfolios almost identical to portfolios chosen by the trust investor. This discovery alone might have subsequently induced the trust investor to alter his decision process, if for no other reason than to be less predictable in order to avoid being replaced by a computer portfolio selection model. This type of phenomena in systems comprised of human beings further complicates the systems analyst's difficulties in understanding the whole system, because the mere act of analyzing its parts may affect the behavior of the system.

Conclusion

In the foregoing comments I have stressed the difficulties of social science research, which in my viewpoint apply as well to accounting research. In conclusion, allow me again to refer to von Mises: "The whole of science can be resolved (in a vague way) into separate sciences, according to the realms of phenomena that each treats. The idea that there exists a fundamental unbridgeable difference in method or even in the kind of 'understanding' between the natural sciences and the humanities is untenable. In history and the social sciences, too, one deals with observations, inductive generalizations, hence theories, and with the first approaches to tautological systems; every result in the last analysis, a proposition verifiable in experience."[10] This, I think, is part of what Professor Churchman is attempting to convey to accountants.

9. Geoffrey P. E. Clarkson, *Portfolio Selection: A Simulation of Trust Investment* (Englewood Cliffs, N.J.: Prentice-Hall, 1962).

10. Von Mises, p. 369.

Prior Accounting Studies

#1 "Financial and Managerial Reporting by Certified Public Accountants"

#2 "Annotated Bibliography of Electronic Data Processing: Updated to December 31, 1967"

#3 "The American Accounting Association–Sponsored Statements of Standards for Corporate Financial Reports–A Perspective" by Harvey T. Deinzer

#4 "Aspects of Contemporary Accounting"

#5 "Methodological Presuppositions in Financial Accounting Models" by Harvey T. Deinzer

#6 "Theory Formulations"

Copies of all Accounting Series issues may be secured from
University of Florida Press
15 N. W. 15th Street
Gainesville, Florida 32601